ALONGSIDE
LOVING TEENAGERS WITH THE GOSPEL

Drew Hill

New
Growth
Press

www.newgrowthpress.com

New Growth Press, Greensboro, NC 27404
Copyright © 2018 by Drew Hill

Many of the names of actual people in this book have been changed, out of respect.

Cover Design: Faceout Books, faceoutstudio.com

ISBN 978-1-945270-89-5 (Print)
ISBN 978-1-945270-90-1 (eBook)

Library of Congress Cataloging-in-Publication Data on file

Printed in China

25 24 23 22 21 20 19 18   2 3 4 5 6

"This book is a gift. I commend it to parents, pastors, lay leaders, and most especially, our fearless heroes: those walking alongside teenagers in youth ministry."
Foley Beach, Archbishop and Primate, The Anglican Church in North America

"*Alongside* is a modern-day primer for parents and youth workers. A must-read for those who are serious about meeting teenagers where they are."
Gail Ebersole, InterVarsity Christian Fellowship, Vice President, Eastern US

"*Alongside* is a great read for any parent or student leader who wants to effectively engage students with the gospel."
J. D. Greear, Pastor of The Summit Church, Durham, NC

"This book will equip anyone to impact the next generation with the heart of God."
Clint Gresham, Seattle Seahawks Super Bowl XLVIII Champion; best-selling author of *Becoming*; international speaker

"*Alongside* takes you on an amazing journey through the struggles and trials of being a teenager . . . A great read!"
Dave Alpern, President, Joe Gibbs Racing

"*Alongside* helps transform the principles of the Gospel into very practical ways to inspire the tender hearts of young people."
Joe White, President of Kanakuk Kamps

"*Alongside* is an essential read for anyone who loves teenagers and seeks to reach their hearts with the gospel."
Matthew Smith, singer-songwriter, Indelible Grace

"This is not just a book about relating to youth culture. It is a road map for living life well, at any age and in any community. Read it. Do what it says. The rewards are generous."
Allen Levi, singer-songwriter; author of *The Last Sweet Mile*

"*Alongside* is a great resource to have on your bookshelf through the seasons of life and ministry."
Cesar Castillejos, Pastor; father; youth ministry veteran

"This book was written in the trenches, years and years of relating to students and parents. . . . It is authentic, relevant, and helpful. A *must* read for anyone leading teenagers!"
Bryson Vogeltanz, Location Pastor, Passion City Church, Atlanta, GA

"Drew Hill not only captures your heart with the power of the gospel, but this book is also full of captivating stories and illustrations. *Alongside* is an excellent resource for the church."
Matthew Z. Capps, Senior Pastor, Fairview Baptist Church, Apex NC

"A must-read book, *Alongside* is refreshingly honest and filled with life-changing, relationship-enriching insights and inspiration."
Fil Anderson, Author of *Running on Empty*

"A must-read for anyone involved in youth ministry."
Jim Branch, Youth ministry veteran; author of *The Blue Book*   .

"Drew Hill's passion for Jesus and teenagers is contagious! *Alongside* is an excellent read. Short, fun to read chapters, packed full of relevant stories and practical ministry ideas."

Bradley J. Widstrom, Associate Professor, Chair Youth and Family Studies, Denver Seminary, Littleton, CO

"Drew starts with Scripture, shares stories about teenagers he's known, and offers practical tools for living out 1 Thessalonians 2:8 with the teenagers in your life."

Julie Clapp, Mission Director of WyldLife, Young Life

"Drew invites parents and youth workers to be a forgiving, redeeming, gospel-centric presence in teenagers' lives and to drink deeply from the power of prayer."

Jodi Chung, Youth Pastor, West Houston Chinese Church, Houston, TX

"I can't wait to share this gem of a book with family, friends and fellow youth workers."

Rich Van Pelt, Compassion International, Senior Director for Ministry Relationships

"Hill is one of the most qualified people to write this diamond of a book. . . . This raw, real, and relevant work will help all who read it find their way, and invest in the next generation."

Pete Hardesty, Young Life College Divisional Coordinator; author of *Adulting 101*

"Whether you're a parent, a church youth minister or volunteer, a teacher, or in any way involved with teenagers, you'll be challenged, inspired, and encouraged."

Ty Saltzgiver, Author of *My First 30 Quiet Times*

"*Alongside* captures the essence of what Drew's life has taught me: God designed his message to live in people. The Word becoming flesh was not an isolated event, but a precedent for all of us."

Zak Ellison, Young Life Area Director, Merced, CA

I truly believe this book should be in every household. It will be practically helpful for parents, teachers, coaches and all those in youth ministry."

Odysseus Wallace, Young Life Area Director, Chattanooga, TN

"As someone in family ministry, *Alongside* is the best of both worlds—a helpful tool that will both build up our volunteers and also serve as an encouragement for parents."

Paul Mannino, Family Pastor, Grace Church, Kutztown, PA

"As an educator of seventeen years, *Alongside* has allowed me to see my students in a more compassionate and loving way!"

Joey Menendez, High School Principal, San Jose, Costa Rica

"*Alongside* helps us mouth words of prayer for young people and invites us into their world through vivid snapshots of unfiltered real-life stories."

Sean McGever, Professor of Theology at Grand Canyon University, Phoenix, AZ; author of YLHelp.com

To Natalie: You show me Jesus.

To Honey, Hutch, and Macy Heart: The treasure is you, you see.

To Mom and Dad: Thank you for loving me with the gospel.

CONTENTS

Part Four: The Long Road Home

INTRODUCTION

Because we loved you so much, we were delighted to share with you not only the gospel of God but our lives as well.

—1 Thessalonians 2:8

LUKE PALMER ran away.

On the surface, it seemed as if everything was normal, but underneath Luke's typical smile was a volcano of stress. A few days before Luke went missing, his teacher called Luke's parents, Eric and Sheila, to arrange a meeting. The teacher wanted to discuss Luke's academic performance.

In his first semester of high school, Luke hadn't been honest with his parents about his grades. It was the day of the dreaded meeting, and although he didn't have his driver's license, the fifteen-year-old knew where his dad's keys were. He wasn't about to wait around for his parents to return home after their meeting with his teacher. As Eric and Sheila pulled down their driveway, driving Sheila's car, they noticed Eric's car was missing. Luke didn't have a phone. There was no way for his parents to know where he was. His dad started calling Luke's friends, who claimed to know nothing, other than the fact that Luke had mentioned the possibility of running away.

Upset and anxious, Eric drove from North Carolina to Virginia searching for his son. He stopped at almost every gas station and rest stop along the highway. Eventually, he returned home empty-handed, begging God for his son's safe return.

In desperation, Eric called the high school principal. The principal talked to some of Luke's friends, who thought he might be heading to New York City, but no one knew for sure. One of Eric's coworkers, David Thompson, suggested they make the road trip to NYC and at least be there in case Luke called. At one thirty on Friday afternoon, Eric and David started driving. They made it to Manhattan by midnight and started the search in Times Square.

In the sea of people, Eric felt no hope of finding his son. David and Eric decided to split up. David walked in one store, then another. No Luke. Then, he walked into the Times Square McDonald's and broke down in tears.

David called Eric. "I'm with Luke."

Like a scene out of a movie, Eric dashed in front of taxis to get across the street. Moments later, he was holding his lost son. This story may seem unbelievable, but it's true.

*****

Twenty-five years before David Thompson had driven to New York with Eric Palmer to chase down Luke, he had pursued a fifteen-year-old in his church's youth group named Drew Hill. Yes, me.

While writing this book, my wife Natalie and I started listing names of people who have pursued us—people who have walked alongside us and demonstrated the gospel, with their lips and their lives. Along with David Thompson, it was quite a list of friends, family members, pastors, teachers, Young Life leaders, mentors, coaches, and bosses. Since the time I learned to run, they made me believe I was worth the chase.

I'm grateful for the countless people who have shown me Jesus, but that doesn't take away my longing to be pursued. I'm almost forty years old and still wrestle with the lies of loneliness that tell me I'm not worth loving.

Our teenage friends and children have the very same longings. They hunger for pursuit. They are desperate to be loved. They crave to be chased.

The adolescent years are ones of great confusion; you might remember your own. Teenagers are trying to figure out who they are, where they belong, and if they matter. They're searching for identity, meaning, and happiness. As Victor Hugo once wrote, "Life's greatest happiness is to be convinced we are loved." Is there anything more convincing than the gospel?

The gospel is the good news that even though we're far worse than we ever imagined, we're far more loved than we could ever dream.[1] God created us in his image, and despite our sin and rebellion, he himself put on skin, came alongside us, and brought his kingdom to earth. In his great love, Jesus took on our human nature, lived a perfect life, bore the cross we deserved, defeated death, and brought us into the presence of God forever.

The gospel is the ultimate answer to the questions and longings of our teenage friends.

"Who am I?" "Where do I belong?" "Do I even matter?"
You are a masterpiece, created in the very image of God. Even though you feel as if you don't deserve his love, through Jesus and his sacrifice on the cross, you are forgiven. You are made righteous and accepted by a holy God. You are so valuable that God himself gave his life for you. You now have the right to be called a son or daughter of God. And as a prince or princess of the King of Kings, you actually get to be an ambassador of God on this earth. You are the light of the world. God has unbelievable plans, and he's invited you into his story. And it's the greatest love story ever told.

Adolescence is such a pivotal time of development. Teenagers are searching for answers to these questions of identity, belonging, and purpose. They are desperately longing for intimacy and acceptance. Every other place they look will only leave them with more brokenness and confusion. Jesus is their only hope.

So, how do we actually share the incredibly good news of Jesus with our adolescent children and teenage friends? How do we lead them toward truth and intimacy with God? How do we love teenagers with the gospel?

In 1 Thessalonians 2:7–8, the apostle Paul gives a compelling example: "Just as a nursing mother cares for her children, so we cared for you. Because we loved you so much, we were delighted to share with you not only the gospel of God but our lives as well."

Sharing the gospel is far more than sharing information. It's opening up our very lives, giving away our very souls. It's unveiling our longings, our fears, our joys. It's inviting others into our mess and being willing to step into theirs.

Paul paints a picture of what the gospel does to the heart. He describes the tenderness of a nursing mother with her child. The gospel leads us into a deep place of holy intimacy where our response is to delight in giving away our very lives.

If you're a parent, youth pastor, Young Life leader, grandparent, coach, teacher, small group leader, or simply anyone who cares about teenagers: This was written for you.

While I may have never met you, I've prayed for *you* while I've written. I have prayed that the pages that follow will stir in you an even greater affection for your children and your middle and high school friends. I have begged God that, somehow, he would use these imperfect sentences to grant you insight into how you can actually walk alongside a teenager. I've asked the Lord that these words might give you a framework and passion for communicating the gospel of grace. And most of all, I've prayed that this book may be a reminder that we have a God who pursues, delights in, and walks alongside us.

Delighted to share,

PART ONE: THE RUNAWAYS

The Story of Teenagers: Those in Need of a Rescue

Teenagers are awesome—a mix of childlike spirits and adultlike ambitions. Knowing them is a gift, but loving them is often challenging. One of the biggest challenges we face is simply understanding and remembering what it's like to be a teenager. That time of transition can feel a lot like leaping from the cliff of childhood, grasping for the mountain of adulthood, and finding yourself stuck in midair. Adolescents need wise, caring adults who are committed to reaching into their worlds, although it often requires taking a leap of faith ourselves.

As a kid, I remember being so frustrated by the *Magic Eye* books my friends brought to school. They claimed if I just stared at the two-dimensional patterns and "went cross-eyed," I could see a three-dimensional image pop out of the picture on the page. It seemed as if everyone else could see it, but no matter how hard I tried, it just looked like a jumbled pattern of different shapes and colors. Then, one day, it just happened. My friends told me to "relax my eyes and get lost in the picture." The next thing I knew, I was screaming like it was Christmas morning. I could finally see the three-dimensional image!

Sometimes it feels as if we try so hard to understand teenagers, only to be slapped in the face with frustration, confusion, and rejection. In this first section, my hope is that you get lost in the world of adolescence—and that somehow, through the grace of God, he would open our eyes to better understand the teenagers in our lives.

CHAPTER 1 || BROKEN HEART

Give me your heart and let your eyes delight in my ways.
—Proverbs 23:26

THERE'S THIS one-act play I've seen a half-dozen times. [1] It opens with a little girl sitting center stage, smiling and holding a big juicy orange that represents her heart.

The narrator begins, "Meet Sally Smith. She is an average, all-American five-year-old girl. Her favorite pastimes are helping Mom in the kitchen, playing with Play-Doh, visiting Grandma, and going to preschool. A fun and exciting life—lots of love and security. But then, one day, things changed."

Sally is told by her mother that her parents are getting divorced. Sally cries, and her mother tries to convince her that everything's going to be OK. Her mother says Sally can visit her dad one weekend each month, and he might even take her to the zoo. Sally, left alone in her room, begins asking hard questions: "Daddy, don't you love me anymore? Did I do something wrong? And Mommy—Mommy, you must not love me either. Otherwise you wouldn't send Daddy away!"

With soft music playing in the background, Sally tears a piece from the orange and throws it in the distance. It feels as if a piece of her heart has been torn apart. In the next scene, a character portraying the devil introduces himself to Sally.

"Sally, I know you don't know me, but I'm your friend. And it sure sounds as if something terrible has happened to you. But don't worry; I've got just what you need. I have some *toys* just for you."

The first toy he gives her is called the *twig of bitterness*. He instructs her to use it to protect her heart. He promises that the little twig will prick anyone who dares to come near. He gives her some nails to protect her as well. A nail of anger—to wound those who hurt her. A nail of jealousy. A rod of blame.

The play continues, and Sally becomes a teenager. She gives her heart away to her high school boyfriend, Mike. Over the years, more and more pieces of the orange are ripped off, and eventually, even Mike doesn't want her ugly heart anymore. When he gives it back, she melts in devastation.

At the end of her rope and not knowing where to turn, the devil shows up again. He reminds Sally about the twig of bitterness and shows her how it's now grown into a full thornbush.

"Use this to protect your heart," he says.

He then gives Sally a pair of headphones and says, "Wear these all the time, stay busy and distracted, and you won't have to think about the pain and loneliness." He takes dark glasses and places them over her eyes, saying, "These negative glasses will give you a whole new perspective on life and show you how things really are!"

Throughout the skit, Jesus comes onto the scene, asking Sally, "Will you let me love you?" Being present, but not pushy. At one point, Sally finally offers him her heart, but when Jesus holds it, because of the thorns pressing in, it hurts her, and she takes it back.

Sally runs to the devil and tells him her heart hurts when people try to love her, so he gives her his *Armor-All protection plan*. He wraps her heart in aluminum foil.

"Now no one can ever hurt you again."

This is usually the point in the play where my eyeballs start to sweat. When I see Sally, I picture so many actual faces of my teenage friends. There they are, negative glasses covering their eyes, headphones covering their ears. In one hand they're holding anger, jealousy, bitterness, and blame—in the other, a broken heart, covered by aluminum foil, not letting anyone in.

As Sally sleeps on the stage, the narrator speaks over the music: "As time goes by, we find Sally run down from all the activities, still with a gnawing dissatisfaction inside. Her toys aren't enough. But she holds onto them because there's no better alternative."

Sally wakes up and wrestles with her thoughts.

I wonder if there's more to life than these toys. Like God or something. I wonder if he even exists. For that matter, I wonder if he even knows I exist. Even if he did, I doubt he'd care about anyone like me. Especially if he knew everything I've done. God? God, I'm afraid of you. I'm afraid of what you might see, and I'm afraid of what you might ask, but if your love is big enough to reach down and . . . ahhh . . . This is stupid. I'm better off playing with my toys and *pretending things are OK than simply talking into the air.*"

Jesus then removes her headphones. "Here, let me take some of the busyness from you. It only keeps you from hearing me. You see, I came to give hearing to the deaf. Sally, let me remove these glasses from you. They distort your vision and keep you from seeing me as I really am. I came to give sight to the blind."

Gradually, Sally surrenders all her toys to Jesus. He then asks for her heart.

"But it's torn and ugly . . . I don't even want you to look at it! Every time I've given my heart away, I've been hurt: my parents, my friends, Mike, even Satan. They all deceived me. How can you expect me to trust you? It's all I have left."

Jesus gently replies, "Because I died for you. Because I love you. There was no other way for you to be free."

As Sally hands Jesus her aluminum-covered heart, he slowly peels back the foil.

Underneath is a brand-new, shiny orange.

"Sally, I came to heal the brokenhearted. The old has gone, the new has come."

*****

Maybe you recognize some of your teenage friends, or even your own children, in the portrait of Sally Smith. Few things are as painful as watching the people you love turn away from the God who loves them.

But this is nothing new. It's been happening since Genesis 3.

Have you ever wondered why loving teenagers is so hard? And why parenting them takes that difficulty to a whole new level? Could it be that the rebellion of our children draws us to more deeply depend upon God? Think about Genesis 3. Adam and Eve rebelled against God, yet even after they were caught, their hearts were not softened to him. What did they do? They covered their shame. Not with aluminum foil, but with fig leaves. They hid. Not in a thornbush, but among the bushes of the garden. They pointed the *rod of blame*—the man toward the woman, and the woman toward the serpent. Then, they were banished from the garden.

In Genesis 4, Adam and Eve become parents. We still see no sign of repentance or the softening of their hearts. Nothing at all . . . until their first-born son killed his little brother. Can you imagine the pain parents would feel if they found out their eldest son had attacked and murdered their baby boy? Can you hear Adam and Eve wailing in the dark of the night, echoing throughout the forest? Is there any deeper despair than that of losing a child?

Near the end of the chapter, it finally happens—the finale of the Adam and Eve narrative. "At that time people began to call on the name of the LORD" (Genesis 4:26). It wasn't until after their children rebelled that Adam and Eve willingly turned to God for help.

Parenting is often painful. Pursuing our teenage friends is downright hard. But through it, God is drawing us to himself. He's saying, "This is way bigger than you, and your giftedness, and your *cool factor*. If you want to do this, you're going to need *me*."

Many of our teenage friends are brokenhearted. I imagine they feel as if they're holding Sally's mangled orange in their stressed-out hands. But the Lord is inviting us to join in with them, right in the middle of that brokenness, to be what Henri Nouwen calls a *wounded healer*[2]—to remove the foil from our own hearts and share with them our shattered souls. To wail in the woods on their behalf.

This isn't a journey for the light of heart. This is war. An enemy is seeking to kill, steal, and destroy our kids. God has called us to fight. Not alone, but with the Divine Warrior leading the charge (see Exodus 15:3).

For Parents

- When have you been vulnerable with your kids? How did that affect your relationship with them?

- What keeps you from being vulnerable with them?

- What would it look like for you to reveal your "mangled orange" to your kids this week? Maybe a coworker or friend recently hurt your feelings. Maybe, even now as an adult, you still struggle with your body image from wounds you suffered as a teenager. Maybe you feel on the outside of the neighborhood's inner circle. How could you show your kids your heart?

- How has being a parent drawn you to depend more on God?

For Those in Youth Ministry

- When kids are hurting, they are often quick to push you away. That's usually when they need love most. Give them space, but don't let rejection keep you from pursuing them. Just because they don't return your texts and calls immediately doesn't mean you should stop pursuing them. Try other ways to care for them. Show up at their games and bring them a cold Gatorade to have afterward. Bring a smoothie by their house. Handwrite notes and leave them on their windshields before school. Patiently come alongside them, even when it seems they're running away.

- What makes it hardest for you to pursue your teenage friends? What holds you back?

- Who is your Sally Smith right now?

- What does it practically look like for you to fight for kids?

The Word of the Lord

"The thief comes only to steal and kill and destroy; I have come that they may have life, and have it to the full" (John 10:10).

A Prayer for Broken Hearts
(Fill in the blanks with the names of the teenagers in your life.)

Father,
You are the Giver of Life. Your hands pumped the heartbeat into my very chest.
You hold my heart tenderly. You heal my heart completely. You alone make it new.
Would you hold and heal _____'s heart?

Jesus,
You are the One whose heart was pierced on the cross.
You understand how it feels when a heart breaks.
Would you come alongside _____
and tend to the wounds that can be found there?

Spirit,
You are the Great Comforter.
And even when I don't know the words to pray, you make sense of my wordless sighs and aching groans.
Would you come and help me pray for _____?
Would you wail in the woods on my behalf?
I need You. I trust You. Amen.

CHAPTER 2 || SOS

I'm reaching out, one last plea
Is hope all gone, somebody save me
SOS I'm lost at sea
Is hope all gone, somebody save me.
—Ed Cash, "SOS"

WHAT YOU'RE about to read is, at times, offensive.

To understand how to communicate the gospel to teenagers, we need to understand the language they speak. The following are actual posts written online by my teenage friends. I've removed their names for privacy and chosen to include most of the original language, including profanities and vulgarities.

- I wish I believed I was worth loving.
- I wasted my childhood trying to grow up.
- I'm screaming at the top of my lungs, and no one even turns their head.
- Why do we live in a world where losing your phone is more dramatic than losing your virginity?
- My sister just texted me *I hate men* . . . she's 12 #WhatTheHECK
- Leave it to me to always *f* everything up.
- Why cancer? Tell me why!
- Dear Mom and Dad, cut it out. I can hear you, and IT'S GROSS.
- I hate when my mom talks about how awesome my brother and sister are #IFeelLikeCrapNow
- Why isn't my dad around? #a**hole
- Why do I constantly feel like the biggest financial burden on my parents? #stress
- I told my mom I'm depressed and can't do my homework cause I'm emotionally damaged. She believed me and is taking me to the doc. #LOL
- Girls are always talking about working out for their "spring break bods" . . . most of y'all are gonna look fat no matter what.

- My parents CONSTANTLY put me down in front of others.
- Crying because I'm so exhausted and I want to sleep but I can't because I have so much work.
- Try walking a mile in my shoes, then u can b*tch at me for not being perfect.
- Thou shalt not ever be pale. #PrettyGirlProblems
- OK, I'm bored. What should I pierce?
- I wish I was close enough with my mom to tell her everything I was feeling right now.
- I hate how trust takes forever to gain and just one stupid thing can make you lose all of it.
- There's no religion that could save me.
- Emotionally . . . I'm done. Mentally . . . I'm drained. Spiritually . . . I feel dead. Yet physically . . . I smile.

Sometimes the cries come in more than 140 characters. One of my high school friends sent me this message. I've received dozens just like it:

Drew,

Last night . . . sh*t hit the fan, and I mean hard. Everything was going good and then my mom had the great idea to start the timeless argument about how I don't care about school. She called me downstairs and logged into the parent portal to check my grades . . . they were bad. I had pretty much given up hope this year.

As the argument continued, I found myself falling into a pit of deep-seeded hatred and anger for my parents. *They just don't get it*, I thought. I punched my wall, 'cause that's what kids do in movies and stuff, but it kinda hurt, and I didn't feel any better.

My dad is so angry. He took away all my stuff. My phone, my laptop, my friends, my driving privileges for, as he said, "the entire summer." He even told my mom to take away all my clothes except for two pairs of shorts, two pairs of shirts, two pairs of socks, and one pair of shoes. He said my life is going to be like the military. We are talking waking up early, doing chores, and yard work every day this summer.

This is the worst ever. Now I know why people become alcoholics. My parents just don't get what I'm going through. They don't understand my emotions. I feel like nobody understands me.

I have lost touch with God. I'm stupid, worthless, scrawny, ugly, too skinny, no girlfriend, and living for no reason.

My parents came in to say good night to me and told me they were sorry, but they did it 'cause they love me. When they said "Goodnight, love you," all I could mumble was, "I wish the feeling was mutual."

Ben

Can you hear it? They're screaming between the lines. Chase me. Pursue me. Reach out to me. Notice me. Rescue me. Save me!

A few years ago, I took a group of high schoolers to a camp in the North Carolina mountains. A special musician was playing for the weekend. That Saturday morning, he was in his cabin, alone with his guitar, and was able to put words to what our teenage friends are feeling. Less than an hour after he wrote the song, we sang it for the first time. It was a holy moment. More than five hundred high schoolers sang the following at the top of their lungs.[1]

> I'm reaching out
> One last plea
> Is hope all gone
> Somebody save me
> SOS, I'm lost at sea
> Is hope all gone
> Somebody save me

I wonder if the kids even realized that when they sang *SOS* it meant *save our souls*. Ed, the camp musician, wrote the following lyrics as the first verse of the song.

> I've been blinded by insecurity
> And all the pain I feel
> Could be the death of me
> I'm surrounded by
> Fear that won't let go
> If there's a way out
> Someone let me know

Why did it resonate with my high school friends? Why did it become a defining anthem for the weekend? Why do those kids still love to sing it?

Through the freedom of musical expression, our teenage friends had been given permission to put their arms around one another and sing with all their might, using words they'd thought they could never say out loud. *Somebody save me.* It's a cry of dependence.

I need help.

But the very essence of adolescence tells teenagers they're supposed to be moving out of that stage, moving from dependence to independence.

I no longer need anyone!

I can do it on my own.

I can be independent.

Our teenage friends feel stuck in the space between. They need adults, who they perceive as independent, to show them that yelling SOS isn't a sign they're drowning, but a sign they're alive.

A few thousand years ago, one of the psalmists cried SOS in Psalm 118:25. He prayed, "Lord, save us!" The original Hebrew words gave us our English word *Hosanna.* In the psalm, *Hosanna* was immediately followed by a shout of hope in verse 26: "Blessed is he who comes in the name of the Lord." It's as if the sinking ship sees the Coast Guard coming at the very moment they shoot the flare.

In the Old Testament, *Hosanna* meant *please save us.* But in the New Testament, it came to have a different meaning. It moved from being a cry for help to a declaration of victory. For hundreds of years, the Israelites had been longing for a king and a deliverer. As Jesus entered Jerusalem during the Passover week, the people lined the streets and shouted those words of victory. "Hosanna! Blessed is he who comes in the name of the Lord!" The Savior they had been longing for had finally arrived.

As we share the gospel with our teenage friends, we get to tell them the truth. We get to show them that crying SOS isn't just a shout of surrender but a declaration of victory. We get to create safe spaces for them to wave their arms like a drowning child and scream, "save me." But we also get to share with them the even better news that *Hosanna* no longer just means *save me.* It now means *salvation has come.* And we get to tell them that salvation has a name. His name is *Jesus.*

For Parents

Consider asking your teenager to join you for a late-night snack before bed. Let him read over the online posts in the preceding pages, written by actual teenagers. Ask your teenager if the posts accurately describe his peers. Ask him to circle any of them he can personally relate to.

Consider sharing as honestly as you can with him. What has Jesus rescued you from? Share about what your most honest online posts might say. Both when you were a teenager and even now. Ask him to pray for you and ask how you can pray for him.

For Those in Youth Ministry

Consider sharing these online posts with your middle and high school friends. You could use it in a talk with your youth ministry or in a small group discussion. You can download PowerPoint and Keynote slides of all the online posts, along with a printable PDF, at AlongsideTeenagers.com.

After you share these posts, consider asking your teenage friends to write down their own. Give them the option to turn them in anonymously or to include their names if they feel so inclined. A helpful question you could ask might simply be, "What do you need Jesus to rescue you from?"

For Both Parents and Those in Youth Ministry

My friend Megan Harvey led a small group Bible study with high school girls in our hometown. One day, I saw her carrying a big stack of journals and asked her about them. She said they were *exchange journals*, and a way for the girls in her group to have a safe space to be completely honest with their thoughts and questions. Each week, at their Bible study, Megan would get them from the girls and take them home to read. She then would write a letter to each of them in the journals, and a couple days later, return their journals when she ate lunch with them at school. The girls would read what Megan wrote and repeat that process every week.

Some pages were filled with doodles and drawings. Others were filled with Scripture verses, written in girly fonts. But some were covered with words, broken hearts spilled out on tear-soaked pages.

It won't work with every single kid, but even though I'm a guy, I would've loved that opportunity for a safe place to share my thoughts and questions during my teenage years. Consider giving exchange journals a shot, either with your own children or those involved in your youth ministry. If you do it, make sure to recognize the bravery in their honesty and praise their willingness to give it a chance.

The Word of the Lord

"It is by the name of Jesus Christ of Nazareth, whom you crucified but whom God raised from the dead, that this man stands before you healed. Jesus is 'the stone you builders rejected, which has become the cornerstone.' Salvation is found in no one else, for there is no other name under heaven given to mankind by which we must be saved" (Acts 4:10–12).

A Prayer of Surrender

Hosanna,
My own efforts continue to fail me, so I lay down my self-sufficiency.
With arms now empty, I wave them like a drowning child.
I cry out to you, "Save me!"
I cry out to you, "Save _____."
I've been blinded by insecurity.
Open my eyes to see through the confident lens of the cross.
_____ has been blinded by insecurity.
Open _____'s eyes to see through the confident lens of the cross.
I've been surrounded by fear that won't let go.
Pry open fear's grip and surround me with angel armies.
_____ has been surrounded by fear that won't let go.
Pry open fear's grip and surround _____ with angel armies.
Jesus, I cry out to you, and declare the victory of your name, *Hosanna*—salvation has come! Amen.

CHAPTER 3 || DEEP END

But when he saw the wind, he was afraid and, beginning to sink,
cried out, "Lord, save me!"
—Matthew 14:30

IT WAS a Thursday night in early July. Many of our friends gathered at the neighborhood pool. Burgers sizzled on the grill and background music from The Zac Brown Band made it feel as though we found our own little paradise. After dinner, we gathered all the sinking rings and wet beach towels and pushed the stroller home. An hour later, we heard the ambulance racing by.

Some of our closest friends had stayed at the pool with their four kids, all under the age of seven. In a split second, with their backs turned in conversation, their two-year-old daughter jumped in. But Anna Claire didn't know how to swim. She happened to drop in directly below the lifeguard stand— just out of view of the very person who had been trained to save her. Another six-year-old girl saw what happened and rushed to tell her mother, Rebecca.

Pointing and in a confused voice, she said, "Mommy, that little girl with blond hair fell under the water and hasn't come up yet."

Without hesitation, and not even knowing who the little girl was, Rebecca raced to the edge of the pool and yanked up sweet Anna Claire. She looked lifeless and blue. A few off-duty doctors and nurses swarmed to her side. An ambulance was there in minutes. After a night in the hospital, by God's grace, Anna Claire went home the next day. No permanent damage had been done.

As a dad of three, I've changed the way I parent at the pool after the night of Anna Claire's accident. Since then, it's been a little harder to relax. I imagine that will change once all our kids learn to swim, but one thing will never change: Whether they're mine or not, there will always be little ones at our pool who don't know how to swim. There will always be kids who are seconds away from drowning.

Dozens of adults were at the pool that night. Any one of them would have done the exact same thing Rebecca did, if only they had noticed that Anna Claire was in trouble.

My guess is that one of the reasons you're holding this book is that you're an adult who *has* noticed. You've noticed children drifting into the deep end without quite knowing how to swim. All of a sudden, the teenagers in your life have transitioned from the shallow end of childhood into the deep end of puberty, and all that goes with it.

You want to reach out. Your heart longs to rescue them. But you also feel overwhelmed and insecure. You wonder if you have what it takes. Anna Claire didn't need an expert swimmer—she just needed a hand. You would never think of watching a little girl drown just because you weren't lifeguard certified. Like Anna Claire, teenagers just need someone who cares, someone willing to show up and reach out. Prior experience is not required.

Last night, I received a text message from a friend who leads a small group of middle school girls:

> Drew, why am I doing this? I can't translate "middle school girl talk." I try really hard to understand these girls, but I don't at all, because my life in middle school looked SO different from theirs. They ask me for advice on things I'm not really equipped to give advice on. I'm too young. I really don't think I have anything to offer them. I'm too inconsistent. And I'm struggling to have the time and patience needed to love them well. They deserve better than that. I just am not sure I should be leading.

Earlier in the day, I had a long conversation with a mother who had recently chaperoned her middle school daughter's field trip. She wanted to process the change she was watching happen in her little girl. To her, it seemed as if they had moved from mother-daughter best buds to complete strangers overnight.

"How can I reach out to her when she just slaps my hand away?"

Being a youth leader, teacher, coach, or anyone who spends time with teenagers can feel a lot like riding a high-speed roller coaster. It's a thrill of a ride, but you often wonder if you're going to survive and why the heck you went to a theme park in the first place. It's hard on the heart.

Parenting teenagers is much the same. The main difference is the roller coaster seems to never stop. Teenagers are intimidating, time-consuming, costly, and messy. If we want to reach them with the gospel—if we want to keep them from drowning—we can no longer simply invite them to come take our class on water safety. Attractional youth programs are not going to get the job done. Parenting lectures typically don't change hearts.

Making disciples is an act that calls for embodied presence. It requires sharing our lives. It demands that we plunge into the deep end—even if we're not convinced *we* know how to swim.

For Parents

I have many fond memories from my days as a young kid at the pool: Marco Polo, cannonball contests, sharks and minnows, and those Nestlé Drumsticks™ with a chunk of chocolate in the bottom of the cone. But something happened around age twelve: the pool got complicated. All of a sudden, I was embarrassed to take off my shirt. I don't think I gained that much weight overnight, or that my skin became any paler. But I do think I saw someone completely different when I looked in the mirror. Someone I didn't like as much.

Adolescence tends to have that effect on children. In a flash, it seems that the early days of splashing in the shallow end come to a screeching halt. Suddenly, teenagers can find themselves drifting to the deep end where it feels much harder to swim.

- Do you remember what that transition from childhood to adulthood felt like? Do you remember the confusion you experienced? Are you showing your child the same grace you wish your parents had shown you? What do you recall about your teenage years?

- When you think about your relationship with your own parents, what do you wish they had done differently to pursue you during your teenage years? Take a minute and write down some of your thoughts here. I wish my own parents would have . . .

For Those in Youth Ministry

- Who reached out to you and helped pull you from the "deep end"? What did they do that affected you?

Maybe no one reached out to you, and you still play the "what if" game in your head. "What if an adult had pursued me when I was a lost teenager?" Now's your chance to give someone that gift you were never given.

The Word of the Lord

"'Come,' he said. Then Peter got down out of the boat, walked on the water and came toward Jesus. But when he saw the wind, he was afraid and, beginning to sink, cried out, 'Lord, save me!' Immediately Jesus reached out his hand and caught him" (Matthew 14:29–31).

A Prayer for Courage

Lion of Judah,
I know if I could see you, my insecurities would sink like a dumbbell in the deep end.
If I was aware that Aslan walked by my side, I could face any foe.
Would you remind me of your powerful presence and be the lifter of my head?
Lamb of God,
You reached out and rescued Peter when he was sinking and afraid.
Would you rescue me too?
Would you help me reach out to _____ and pull your beloved from the water?
Give me the courage of a lion and the meekness of a lamb, so that I may bear your image rightly and boldly surrender to you. Amen.

CHAPTER 4 || HIJACKED

Your beauty and love chase after me every day of my life.
—Psalm 23:6 MSG

SOON AFTER we'd become parents, my wife Natalie and I went to see a low-budget movie[1] on the recommendation of a friend. The opening scene had me holding my breath.

The main character, Nathan, pulls up to a gas station driving a top-of-the-line, extended cab pickup truck. He fills up his tank and cranks the engine to leave. Right before jumping back in the truck, at the last minute, he decides to clean the bugs off his windshield. There's no water in the bucket. He grabs the squeegee and walks over to the next pump to get it wet. When he turns around, he sees a car thief hijacking his truck and screeching away.

Like a madman, Nathan leaps onto his truck, hanging on to the steering wheel through the open driver's side window. The thief pulls on Nathan's arm, trying to pry it off the steering wheel, all while swerving and speeding down a busy road. Ultimately, Nathan is tossed to the ground just as the hijacker smashes the truck into a tree. For a moment, everything is still.

The thief quickly wakes up after the crash and escapes on foot, while Nathan gradually begins to move. Traffic is stopped. Cars pull over. Bystanders call 911.

Nathan attempts to crawl toward the vehicle, and a concerned woman begs, "Sir, just lie still. Don't worry about the car."

Nathan pulls himself up and firmly responds, "I'm not worried about the car." He grabs the handle of the back door, and as it swings open, we see his newborn son—screaming in fear but unharmed in his car seat.

Only two minutes into the movie, at the sound of the baby's cry, tears started flowing in the theater. Now everything made sense. Seconds earlier, I was thinking, "It's just a truck, it's not worth dying over. Let it go, bro!" But seeing that little baby boy, so innocent, so scared—there was absolutely no question that he was worth the chase.

We live in a world that is hijacking the innocence of teenagers. Their hearts are constantly being *abandoned, distracted, and rejected.* While post-Christian culture makes it difficult for us, as adults, to share the gospel with teenagers, that's no excuse to just stand there at the pump and watch the truck pull away. There's precious cargo in the back—and it's worth the chase.

Abandoned

Apart from the problem of sin, I'm convinced the number-one problem facing teenagers today is broken relationships with their parents. But it doesn't stop with parents. It seems one of the unwritten rules for many teenagers is they're not supposed to trust any adult, period.

When I was in high school, a rough-around-the-edges tenth grader named Wyatt showed up at our Wednesday night youth group. I didn't know him—we went to different schools—but we ended up sitting beside each other that evening. As we started singing "Lord I Lift Your Name on High," I turned and asked him who he came with. Decades later, I still remember his response: "I just came on my own. I got kicked out of my youth group, so I'm looking for a new one."

I only heard Wyatt's side of the story, but it was obvious he had been deeply wounded by his church and was hungry for a place to belong. He kept coming back on Wednesday nights, but never really got close with our youth leaders. It would be awhile before he would be willing to trust an adult again.

In the past month, Natalie and I have had two of our friends, both adult women, separately share with us about how they were sexually abused as children—one by her father, another by an adult she trusted.

Teenagers have a hard time trusting adults. They've been wounded by them. Embarrassed by them. Abandoned by them.

As a safeguard, it's almost instinctual to look with suspicion on anyone who seems to care. Teenagers want people who will love them without leaving them—people who will see their messy hearts and not try to fix them.

It's going to take time and understanding for us to earn that trust back. We have to acknowledge that they've been lied to and wounded. We have to admit our own broken places and face the reality that many of us, as adults, are still dealing with our own abandonment issues.

Maybe for you it's a father wound. Maybe you were betrayed by a friend. As we look into our own messes, it makes it easier to understand what our teenage friends might be feeling. And as we share our messes with them, it makes it possible for them to share theirs with us.

Distracted

The culture that's currently raising our teenagers is not the same as the world that raised you and me. The pressures and distractions of this generation are only gaining steam. Yes, they are stressed out by many of the same pressures that affected past generations—pressures to perform on the field, the stage, and the classroom. But now it's magnified because their performance is broadcasted in real time online. They are encountering challenges as teenagers that past generations did not deal with until they were in their midtwenties. It's as if age fifteen is the new twenty-five.

Sure, teenagers are still asking the same questions we asked during our pubescent years: Who am I? Do I matter? Do I belong? Do you like me? Where do I fit in? Why am I here? But they're finding their answers in places that didn't exist twenty years ago. With the introduction of social media and Google in our pockets, they're constantly connected to the world.

But that "connection" can feel more entangling than encouraging. After all, it is called the World Wide *Web*. It's as if our adolescent friends are having to learn how to live in a different country. To reach them, we first have to learn to speak their language.

Rejected

No matter how old you are, I bet you still remember those painful words that were spoken to you as a kid—words that even now can wrestle you to the ground as you stare into the mirror. *You're fat. You're ugly. You're lazy.* You fill in the blank.

Our teenage friends are experiencing the same feelings, only they don't have to search Google. With the tap of a screen, they can log into any of their social media accounts and see exactly how much they're worth. It's determined by the number of likes on their pictures and the number of followers on their profiles. And the ratio is crucial. You *must* have more followers than the number of people you are following.

I've noticed a trend online with my female middle and high school friends. They'll post a picture, right hand on their hip, left knee slightly bent. That's supposedly the best way to look skinnier in a photo (I might give it a shot in our family's next Christmas card). After they post the picture, they'll wait. Then they'll check the likes and the comments, and check over and over again.

And then it will happen. Like clockwork. It always does. Another girl will write, *You're gorgeous!* in the comments. The original picture poster will respond, *No, you are gorgeous!* A different gal will chime in, *I so want to be you.* And so on, and so on.

When a teenage girl writes the words *You are so beautiful,* she's likely asking more of a question: Do you think I'm beautiful too?

During a season in which they're experiencing drastic bodily changes like never before, the world gets to vote on just how attractive they are. They're hungry for approval, affirmation, and affection. They're dying to find out the answer to the question that owns their thoughts, day in and day out: Do you like me?

Not *Do you love me?* but *Do you like me? Do you want to be with me? Do you want to know me? And once you get to know me, the real me, will you still like me, or will you reject me too?*

Our teenage friends have questions. And the places they're looking for answers often leave them feeling even more rejected and confused.

But there is hope. Even when *we* abandon them, there is One who never leaves (Hebrews 13:5).

Even when *we* break their trust, there is One who is always faithful (1 Corinthians 1:9).

Even when *we're* too exhausted to hear their cries, there is One who never slumbers or sleeps (Psalm 121:4).

We have the incredible privilege to tell our young friends the true story of a God who comes to rescue his children. When we were hijacked by sin, he laid down his very life for us. And he is still chasing us today with a "never stopping, never giving up, unbreaking, always and forever Love."[2]

For Parents

- What are the lies you still hear that were spoken over you as a child? Have you ever shared those with your teenager?

- When have you felt abandoned, distracted, or rejected? Have you ever asked your children when they have felt that way? That's not usually a conversation topic that just pops up on the way home from school. It could start with a note from you to them. Maybe something like this:

Noah,

I was lying in bed last night and reading a book that started to make me think about our relationship. I realize there's so much about me I've actually never shared with you. I would love a chance to tell you more of my story, especially the things I went through when I was around your age. If you're willing, I'd love to have dinner with you, just you, on Thursday night. I'll pick the dinner spot, you pick dessert. Please check yes, no, or maybe and leave on my pillow.

Don't force the questions on the same night you share your story. Give it time. Once they see your willingness to be real, their shells will eventually start to crack.

For Those in Youth Ministry

• When have you felt abandoned or betrayed? Have you ever shared that with your middle or high school friends?

• What distracts you from paying attention to the Lord? What are some specific ways you can live differently from the world and set an example for the teenagers in your life in regard to typical distractions of the culture?

• Where have you looked for acceptance? What are some practical ways you can look to the Lord instead of the world?

- Who do you know who is being "hijacked" by the world? What would it practically look like for you to start chasing after them this week?

The Word of the Lord
"But while he was still a long way off, his father saw him and was filled with compassion for him; he ran to his son, threw his arms around him and kissed him" (Luke 15:20).

A Chasing Prayer

Heavenly Father,
When I run away from you, you chase after me.
You call my name and say, "Be still, my child. Know that I am God."
So now, in this very moment, I am stopping.
Like a toddler who ran from a father, I am stopping.
I am waiting for you to catch me. To capture me. To hold me.
In your presence alone will I find true rest.
And this I pray too for _____.
That they will know you as the hound of heaven, the chasing God.
Even when _____ feels abandonment,
may _____know you adopt your children.

Even when _____ is too distracted to notice you, may you speak reminders that your eyes never turn away.
Oh Father, run to _____. Throw your arms around your beloved and kiss them.
Oh marvelous God who runs. There is none like you. Amen.

PART TWO: THE PURSUER

The Story of the Gospel: A God Who Pursues His Runaways

There's a Michael Jackson cover band playing a concert in our hometown this weekend. I think if I could have one superpower, it would simply be to dance like the King of Pop. Although I did learn to moonwalk in middle school (and can still do it if I'm wearing wool socks on a recently polished linoleum floor), the reality is that no matter how many dance lessons I take, no matter how many instructional YouTube videos I watch—even if I bought a black hat and one white glove—I could never move like MJ.

But God, on the other hand—he's a different story. He sent his Son to earth to convey to us the message that we actually can do the very things he can do.

In fact, Jesus said, "Whoever believes in me will do the works I have been doing, and they will do even greater things than these" (John 14:12). Now, either Jesus is a liar, or what he said is absolutely true.

As we communicate the gospel to teenagers, the good news is that we don't have to do it alone. We don't have to settle for being mere copies of God, but we can actually carry the very presence of God himself into the world. We have been given the light of the Son, the delight of the Father, and the comfort of the Holy Spirit.

You're likely holding this book because you want to be better equipped to share the good news of salvation with the young people in your life. This section of the book clearly lays out the gospel and serves as a reminder that because of God's presence with us, we already have everything we need. As we pursue teenagers, we go *with* the Great Pursuer, the One who walks alongside of us.

"Your beauty and love chase after me every day of my life" (Psalm 23:6 MSG).

CHAPTER 5 || THE INCARNATION

The Word became flesh and blood, and moved into the
neighborhood.

—John 1:14 MSG

I READ an article about an elementary school teacher in Texas who taught children who were visually impaired. In an effort to help the parents of those children understand exactly how their kids viewed the world around them, the teacher had an eye doctor make special pairs of glasses, based on the specific eyesight of each student. As she met with parents for teacher conferences, she would ask them to try on the glasses. Then, she would show them a movie clip and ask them to try and read a book.

"This is what it is like for your child every single day of their lives. This is what they see," she said.

We can only imagine the amount of tears that fell during those parent-teacher conferences. What a gift it was for parents to be able to step into their kids' shoes and understand a little more what it must be like to be kindergartners who cannot make sense of what they are seeing. I wonder how it changed those families. I wonder how it deepened the relationship between those parents and their children.

Empathy awakens compassion.

In the opening chapter of the Gospel of John, we find one of the most shocking sentences in all of Scripture: "The Word became flesh and made his dwelling among us" (John 1:14). In the flesh. *In carnes. The incarnation.*

The God of the universe did more than just try on a pair of glasses. He became blind. He didn't merely dip his feet in the water. He dove headfirst into the deep end of our lives.

He became one of us. The God-man, Jesus, the second person of the Trinity, became 100 percent human. Fully God. Fully man. He bridged the gap between created and uncreated beings. He endorsed the very goodness of his own creation. God put on skin. Paul describes it in Philippians 2:5–8 (PHILLIPS):

Christ Jesus: Who, being in very nature God, did not consider equality with God something to be used to his own advantage; rather, he made himself nothing, by taking the very nature of a servant, being made in human likeness. And being found in appearance as a man, he humbled himself by becoming obedient to death—even death on a cross!

He experienced everything we experience:

- He was born as a baby in the humblest conditions.
- He relied upon his parents to take care of him.
- He had brothers and sisters.
- He went through puberty.
- He ate.
- He slept.
- He spent decades in obscurity.
- He battled temptation.
- He lost loved ones.
- He wept.
- He never married.
- He was betrayed by friends.
- He was falsely accused.
- He was persecuted unfairly.
- He suffered in the most horrifying way possible.
- The God of the universe, walking among the very people he created. Why? Because of his love for us. Because he longed to be with us.

A few years ago, a friend of mine was working at a summer camp. One particular week, he happened to have a pretty rough crowd of kids coming through. On the second day, he separated the guys and gals to have some deeper discussion. The guys spent time talking about what it meant to be a man, and at the end, he invited the boys to turn in any weapons or contraband they'd brought with them.

Just as they were finishing up, a smaller high school guy walked up on stage and asked the speaker if he would wait for just a minute. He ran back to his cabin and came back with one of those Nike string bags. Standing on the stage, he opened the bag and dumped out a stack of blue bandanas. He told the speaker he brought those to camp with a plan of recruiting kids to his gang back home.

Later in the week, there was a traditional *Say-So*, where kids stand up and share if they've begun a relationship with Jesus. That same young man stood up, with his leader beside him.

He shared, "I came here with this, but I'm going home with Jesus." At that moment, he dropped his last blue bandana to the ground.

But if you know anything about gang life, it's not that easy to just say you're dropping out. Traditionally, when you join a gang, you take a pretty serious beating as part of your initiation. The idea is that once you're in, you're in for life, so in turn, if you do decide to leave, there's an even more intense beating to endure.

The leader who brought this young man to camp knew what was coming his way when he got home. People were already talking about it going down. But, during the week, the leader had been sharing with his high-school friend how Jesus had suffered for us on the cross and taken our place, so in an act of embodying the gospel, he offered to go with the young man to face his fate. While he couldn't take the young man's punishment *for* him, he vowed to take it *with* him.

Jesus came to earth to enter in with us. In the person of Christ, God revealed what it looks like to love people with relentless pursuit.

The apostle Paul was one of the many people whose life was turned upside down by Jesus Christ. He was radically changed. Even his very name. This man who was named *Saul* had persecuted Christians. After encountering Jesus, *Paul* became the greatest missionary the world has ever known. He describes it this way in 1 Corinthians 9:19–23 MSG:

> Even though I am free of the demands and expectations of everyone, I have voluntarily become a servant to any and all in order to reach a wide range of people: religious, nonreligious, meticulous moralists, loose-living immoralists, the defeated, the demoralized—whoever. I didn't take on their way of life. I kept my bearings in Christ—but I entered their world and tried to experience things from their point of view. I've become just about every sort of servant there is in my attempts to lead those I meet into a God-saved life. I did all this because of the Message. I didn't just want to talk about it; I wanted to be in on it!

The God of the universe is inviting you and me to "be in on it"—to not just talk about Jesus, but to actually enter their world and experience things from their point of view.

For Parents

• What could you do to "put on your child's glasses" and step into their shoes? How could you better understand what they're experiencing and feeling?

• Do you remember any of your emotions from your own days as a teenager? Allow those memories and emotions to help you enter in with your own kids.

For Those in Youth Ministry

• How can we practically enter into the world of our middle and high school friends?

• Do you spend more of your time with teenagers saying "Come to me/my thing" or "Let me come to you"?

The Word of the Lord

"The Son is the image of the invisible God, the firstborn over all creation" (Colossians 1:15).

A Prayer of Confidence (adapted from Hebrews 4:14–16)

God the Father,

On my knees now, I approach your throne of grace.

I do not come to you in my own merit, or in my own worth, or in my own name.

I come to you in the name of your Son, Jesus Christ, my High Priest.

I am coming to you because Christ loved me, died for me, rose for me, and intercedes on my behalf.

With great confidence, I open my hands to receive what you are so ready to give.

I gladly receive this mercy that you so generously offer.

Like Jesus, I ask that you would allow me to be a servant to the world around me.

Would you give me humility?

Would you give me everything I need?

I ask this that I may be able to enter into _____'s life as Christ has entered into mine.

Boldly I ask. Boldly I come. Amen.

Now, the incarnation isn't just the story of Jesus. The incarnation is a three-person gift. God, the Father, sent Jesus, the Son, and—by power of the Holy Spirit—Jesus became flesh. All three persons of the Godhead play significant roles in our understanding of the gospel and of how we share that gospel with teenagers. Over the next three chapters, we'll look at each person of the Trinity and how God comes alongside of us.

CHAPTER 6 || THE LIGHT OF THE SON

> If you want to get warm you must stand near the fire: if you want to be wet you must get into the water. If you want joy, power, peace, eternal life, you must get close to, or even into, the thing that has them.
>
> —C. S. Lewis, *Mere Christianity*

ENTERING THE world of teenagers can be terrifying. Thankfully, we don't just follow Jesus's example but as we enter their world, we actually go with his power. Just as Jesus has pursued us, he now lives in us. And through us, he pursues others. It's a mind-boggling mystery.

We can try and muster up the energy to be good people, good parents, and good youth leaders, but eventually, we'll burn out. If we're simply trying to emulate Jesus's example, we will constantly fail and ultimately give up. Moralism leads to exhaustion.

But if we are filled with the presence of Christ, we are empowered to pursue others with a fire that won't burn out. In the Sermon on the Mount, when Jesus calls us "the light of the world," he uses the illustration of a lamp. Can a lamp produce light on its own? No. A lamp carries the light. We are holders of the light. We don't have to try and shine brighter. We don't have to produce the light. We already possess it.

In the first chapter of John, the beloved disciple writes this:

> In the beginning was the Word . . . In him was life, and that life was the light of all mankind. The light shines in the darkness, and the darkness has not overcome it. There was a man sent from God whose name was John . . . He himself was not the light; he came only as a witness to the light. The true light that gives light to everyone was coming into the world. (John 1:1, 4–6, 8–9)

And then, in Matthew 5:14, the One whom John described as *the true light* tells his disciples of their true identity: "You are the light of the world."

If you are in Christ, the Light of the World is in you. In the Sermon on the Mount, Jesus is talking to his followers, and he starts by telling them who they are: "You are the light." Not "you should be"—but *you are*! It's a statement of fact, voiced by the Son of God, regarding our identity.

But, so often we let the voices of the world determine our identity and our calling. We let our fears scream so loudly that they drown out the voice of Jesus:

- I don't know enough. What if I can't answer their questions?
- I don't have enough time. Where can I fit this into my already busy schedule?
- I'm not cool enough. What if they reject me?
- I'm not put together enough. What if I'm exposed as a hypocrite?

The fears might seem legitimate, but none of them account for the fact that the Light of the World resides within us! We get so caught up focusing on the fears that we forget the good news of the gospel.

"While we were still sinners, Christ died for us" (Romans 5:8). He died for us *while* we were sinners. The power of Christ is made perfect in our weakness, not in our perfection. Jesus opens the Sermon on the Mount with the words, "Blessed are the poor in spirit, for theirs is the kingdom of heaven" (Matthew 5:3). We share the gospel not as people who have it all together, but as people who are "poor in spirit."

Perhaps this short story I wrote for my own children can help illustrate.

The Beggar's Light

There once was a band of beggars who were living in poverty. They were always freezing and hungry and slept on the stone streets of a cold, dark town. It was the only life they knew.

One particularly cold evening, a stranger showed up wildly excited and begged the beggars, saying, "You must come and see what I've found!"

With the zeal of a toddler on Christmas morning, the stranger grabbed their hands and began to run. Before the beggars knew it, they were dashing down a dark alleyway, zigzagging to a part of town they never knew existed. All of a sudden, when the beggars turned the corner, they immediately had to cover their eyes.

At the end of the street was a blazing bonfire, surrounded by dozens of people who sounded as if they were laughing, singing, and celebrating. Uncertain at first, they hesitantly approached. Never before had they felt that kind of heat. Never before had they been exposed to a light so bright. As they drew near to the fire, their eyes slowly began to adjust. And for the first time in forever, they removed their hats, coats, and gloves.

Oh, to feel the warmth of that fire! Oh, to see the light of one another's faces for the very first time! In the presence of the fire, the beggar's bodies began to thaw. Feeling returned to their fingers and toes. They could finally see. They could've sat there forever.

After some time, a kind old man came close. The beggars recognized his voice, for he had been the one leading the chorus of songs earlier in the night. With a gentle breath, he asked their names. The light seemed to reflect off his face as the moon reflects the sun. With a grin of delight, he listened to their stories and nodded as if he understood exactly what they were describing. It oddly felt as if they'd known him their entire lives.

The beggars and the kind old man talked together for what felt like minutes, but surely was hours. Then, the gentleman slowly stood to his feet. Leaning on a cane he'd whittled from a stick, he asked a question. "Do you have any friends or family who are still back home?" After hearing about all their loved ones who they'd left behind, he stuck two handfuls of torches into the fire. After every torch was lit, he carefully handed each of the beggars their own flame. The light was so bright that the beggars could no longer actually see the fellow who had handed them out. It was as if he'd disappeared before their very eyes.

With great eagerness and absolutely no delay, they knew what must happen next. Together, they departed in joyful song and hurried back the same way they had come. The beggars couldn't wait to share the light.

*****

We take the gospel to our teenage friends—not as independent adults who have it all figured out, but as beggars helping other beggars find food. We don't cry, "You heathen, come be more enlightened like me!" Instead, we ask a question: "Are you tired, hungry, cold, homeless, broke, or thirsty? Me too! Come and see where I found rest, food, and warmth. Let me show you where I found belonging, incredible riches, and the place where my thirst was finally quenched. Let me introduce you to the One who is rest, the One who is the Bread of Life, the One who is the Light of the World, the One who is the Prince of Heaven, and the One who is the Living Water—*Jesus Christ*!

The reason Paul was so delighted to share the gospel was that he had experienced this person firsthand. He had known the darkness and had seen the Light. But he hadn't just seen it. The Light had taken up residence within his very being. Now, he knew his true identity as a holder of the Light. And he penned it in a chorus that still sings of that truth almost two thousand years later: "Christ in you, the hope of glory" (Colossians 1:27).

For Parents

- What voices do you let determine your identity? Who tells you what is true about you?

- What are some practical ways you can remind your children of their true identity?

- Do you remember when your eyes were first opened to Jesus? Have you ever told your kids about that experience?

For Those in Youth Ministry

- What are the fears that keep you from sharing the gospel with teenagers?

- What would you do if you believed that the Light of Christ had taken up residence inside of you?

The Word of the Lord

"For God, who said, 'Let light shine out of darkness,' made his light shine in our hearts to give us the light of the knowledge of God's glory displayed in the face of Christ" (2 Corinthians 4:6).

A Prayer for Light

O Great Light of the World,
Without you, life is full of darkness, but you pull open the blinds of my soul and usher dawn into the night.
Without you, life is full of uncertainty and fear, but your steadfast hand stills my shaking heart.
Without you, life is full of confusion, but your perfect Word illuminates truth.
O Great Light of the World, draw back the curtains from my eyes. Emblazon me with the fire that cannot be extinguished by insecurities, discouragement, busyness, or fear.
And as you vanquish the darkness, grant that I may lead
_____ into your marvelous light. Amen.

CHAPTER 7 || THE DELIGHT OF THE FATHER

The Lord your God is with you, the Mighty Warrior who saves.
He will take great delight in you; in his love he will no longer rebuke
you, but will rejoice over you with singing.

—Zephaniah 3:17

WHEN NATALIE and I were going through premarital counseling, we met with our pastor and his wife in their home. We'd sit in their living room and were often interrupted by their kids. It seemed as if their teenage boys were always running in and out of the house. They would come home from school, grab a snack, and then head back out to sports practices and guitar lessons. Every single time they'd walk out that front door, Ken and Sally would say this one specific phrase to them—something we now say to our own children almost every night at bedtime: "I love you, not because of anything you do, but just because you're mine."

There's something about that phrase that just kind of makes your shoulders relax.

"You mean, I don't have to do anything to impress you, to earn your love? You love me regardless?"

But, that's not typically how we live. So much of our lives are spent trying to earn love and acceptance. It's why, even as adults, we're tempted to check the number of likes and followers on our social media accounts. It's one of the reasons we want salary raises—so we can physically see exactly how much we're worth. But the gospel turns that value system completely upside down. The Father's delight in us and his approval of us is not determined by the performance or popularity, but rather by our position as children of God.

How do we know how God feels about his children? Listen to the words he spoke over his son at Jesus's baptism:

He saw God's Spirit—it looked like a dove—descending and landing on him. And along the Spirit, a voice: "This is my Son, chosen and marked by my love, delight of my life." (Matthew 3:16–17 MSG)

Imagine if you had been there the moment when Jesus was baptized. A thirty-year-old carpenter from Nazareth emerges from the water, and suddenly, everyone freezes. A booming voice shakes the sky: "That's my boy!" And then you watch as the hand of God writes #ProudDad in the clouds.

So why does it matter for us that God, the Father, declares his delight in his Son? Because of the work Jesus accomplished on the cross, we can now become Jesus's brother. We can now share his Father. We are invited into the love that is displayed between the Trinity at Jesus's baptism.

Becoming a son or daughter of God is not an additional identifier on the end of our name; it is our new, primary identity. More than twenty times in the New Testament, we're reminded that we are God's children. And as children of God, we must remember that the Father's delight in us is not based on our behavior, but on our brother's. Jesus lived a perfect life and voluntarily traded places with us on Calvary, taking on our sin and, in turn, giving us his righteousness and status as a child of God.

We live in a world that offers conditional delight. If you do this, if you look this certain way, if you perform, if you produce—then you will receive favor. Our heavenly Father's love for us isn't determined by how good of parents we are or how effective we are in youth ministry.

To be God's child is synonymous with being *one whom he delights in*. The voice of God says the same thing to us that Ken and Sally told their teenage sons: "I love you, not because of anything you do, but just because you are mine."

But God even goes one step further than *I love you*. Matthew 3:17 records that a voice from heaven said, "This is my Son, whom I love; with him I am well pleased."

Not only does he love us, but he likes us. He isn't just putting up with us; he is pleased with us.

One summer, I was the work crew boss at a camp in Jasper, Georgia. The speaker for the week was a kind man named Mark, about the same age as my father. I'll never forget one question I heard him ask a room full of teenagers.

Standing on the stage, he started sharing about his children. Mark proudly showed a picture of his eldest son, a successful businessman in New York who was married with kids. Next, he put his middle daughter on the overhead screen. She was beautiful, in her midtwenties, had received a full scholarship to college, and now was working with a senator on Capitol Hill. Finally, he began to describe his youngest daughter. There was no picture to go with his words.

"Our youngest daughter, Maria, is twenty-two and has the IQ of a four-year-old. She has severe mental and physical disabilities and will never be able to live on her own. She will never be able to marry, have a job, play sports, or even use the bathroom by herself."

Then, he asked the question. I can still hear his voice saying the words.

"Do you think I love Maria any less because she'll never be able to do those things?" It was followed by a long pause. "Not at all. I love her . . . simply because she's my little girl."

Then, he blew a kiss to the back of the room. We all turned our heads. There was Maria, sitting in her wheelchair. Her face was beaming as she smiled back at her daddy.

"That's my little girl!"

He wasn't just saying, "I love you, Maria," as a nice compliment. He was shouting to the masses with his face and his words: "I delight in my daughter! Regardless of her performance. She is a reflection of me, and there's nothing that would ever make me want to disown her. Even on her darkest day. I am not more proud of her when she 'performs' better or less proud when she 'fails.' The sense of pride and joy I have in her is completely out of her control. I want to be identified with her and shout from the mountaintop that she is *mine*!"

Do you believe God delights in you like that? Once we become convinced of his delight in us, we will naturally be spring-loaded to share the gospel with others. To get out there and take the light that has been given to us and carry it into the dark and cold places that have never known that love.

It's completely different from being motivated by duty or guilt. It's simply a natural overflow of looking in the mirror and realizing the unbelievable reality: We are children of the living God, and he looks upon us with the tender delight of a Father.

For Parents

- Do you ever feel as though your affection for your children is based upon how they behave or perform?

- Do you believe God could look at you with this delight?

- What people in your life have made it clear they delight in you? Take a moment and thank God for revealing his delight in you through them.

- Make it your goal this week to communicate your love and delight to your kids. Consider using this phrase: "I love you, not because of anything you do, but just because you are mine." They can't hear you say it enough.

For Those in Youth Ministry

- What is your relationship with your earthly father like?

- How does that relationship affect the way you love others?

• Do you treat teenagers differently based on how they perform? Do you feel tempted to show favoritism or extra attention to kids who are easier to love?

• What people in your life have made it clear they delight in you? Take a moment and thank God for revealing his delight in you through them.

The Word of the Lord

"See what great love the Father has lavished on us, that we should be called children of God! And that is what we are!" (1 John 3:1).

A Prayer for Delight

Abba Father,
I desperately need help believing that you not only love me but also delight in me.
I confess to you that I often feel as though I disappoint you and, in turn, wallow in a sea of self-condemnation.
I surrender to you these critical thoughts about myself and beg you to daily remind me of your delight.
Thank you that your love for me and delight in me is completely out of my control.
Oh, what love you have lavished on me, that I should be called a child of God.
Abba Father, may you lavish that same love on
_____.
Grant that I may love others in a way that reflects your delight in them.
I am wholly yours. Amen.

CHAPTER 8 || THE COMFORT OF THE SPIRIT

I will ask the Father, and he will give you another advocate to help you and be with you forever—the Spirit of truth. The world cannot accept him, because it neither sees him nor knows him. But you know him, for he lives with you and will be in you.
—John 14:16–17

ONE OF my favorite people in the world is only eleven years old. I've known him for most of his life and feel a similar affection for him as a father toward a son. Recently, I took a long road trip to visit him in another state. Sadly, for the past three months, he's had to be under constant care in a specialized hospital. It's a lockup facility that specializes in mental, physical, and emotional issues in both children and teenagers.

As I approached his particular unit to check him out for the day, the first thing I noticed was a small square window in the door. Behind it, a dozen young boys were staring out. It was clear from the looks in their eyes that they were all hoping for the same thing. Hoping that the next person to come to the door would be coming for them. Their eyes screamed with the same fears that so many of our teenage friends feel every single day—fears of abandonment, loneliness, isolation, and rejection.

When I read the Gospels and think about Jesus's disciples, I tend to picture them as guys in their thirties, but they weren't. Historical evidence points to them being merely teenagers.[1] Jesus, after all, was only thirty years old when he began his earthly ministry, and these guys were his pupils for the next three years. These twelve ragamuffins dropped everything to follow Jesus, and then in John 14, Jesus drops a bomb.

"Guys, I'm leaving."

Doubting Thomas responded the same way our three-year-old does whenever I'm heading out of town. "Where are you going? I wanna go too!"

Jesus countered with some of the most comforting words that have ever been spoken. They are the words my favorite eleven-year-old needs to hear. The words our teenage friends need to hear, and the very words we need to hear as we pursue the young people in our lives.

And I will ask the Father, and he will give you another advocate to help you and be with you forever—the Spirit of truth. The world cannot accept him, because it neither sees him nor knows him. But you know him, for he lives with you and will be in you. (John 14:16–17)

Sharing the gospel with our middle- and high-school friends can feel overwhelming and downright scary. It can easily surface our own fears of isolation and rejection. Some of my loneliest hours have been spent in high school cafeterias.

But the comforting words that Jesus spoke to his disciples are as true for us today as they were two thousand years ago. Jesus wants us to know that the Great Pursuer always goes with us.

When you're about to have that awkward conversation with your children about the birds and the bees—when you're sitting in their bedrooms and as nervous as you were on your own first day of middle school—Jesus is reminding you that you are not alone.

When you're walking down the halls of the high school and see absolutely no familiar faces—when you feel as out of place as a mouse on a cat farm—Jesus is reminding you that you are not alone.

When you're sitting by the lake at camp and your teenage friend is asking you hard questions about the gospel that you don't feel equipped to answer, Jesus is reminding you that you are not alone.

When you're a single mom trying to raise a teenage boy and you're at the end of your rope, Jesus is reminding you that you are not alone.

Jesus is saying the same thing to us that he so affectionately spoke to his disciples: "I know you're afraid, but take your eyes off of yourself for a minute, and *look at me*. I've got incredible news for you. Yes, I'm leaving, but you won't be alone."

It's crazy to think that at the time Jesus spoke these words, he was well aware that twenty-four hours later he would be nailed to a cross and buried in a tomb. And yet, his last breaths were not focused on his own fears but on comforting ours.

He didn't just speak the comfort but lived it out. Right before he spoke these words in John 14, he got on his hands and knees and washed his disciples' feet. In a position of great humility, he asked them the same question he's asking you and me right now. Will you let yourself be loved by the Lord? And in John 14:16–17, he tells us one of the most significant ways he wants to love us, by giving us a gift. A gift that will be with us no matter where we go, no matter what we face. The gift of himself. The gift of the Holy Spirit. "I will ask the Father, and he will give you another advocate to help you and be with you forever—the Spirit of truth."

This is one of the few places in Scripture where all three members of the Trinity are clearly present in one single verse. *Jesus* asks the *Father* to give the *Holy Spirit* to his disciples. He nicknames the Holy Spirit the *Paraclete*, which in Greek is a combination of two words—*para*, meaning *alongside*, and *klētos*, meaning *called*.

One called to your side is translated a dozen different ways by biblical scholars: Helper, Encourager, Advocate, Counselor, True Friend, and the One Who Comes *Alongside*.

It's important for us to understand exactly what it means, because this word is the primary way Jesus is describing the Holy Spirit. Historically, the word was used to describe someone who stood with another person who was under a great deal of pressure. Some scholars compare it to a lawyer standing with someone on trial, but maybe a more helpful picture would be of a doula during childbirth.

A decade ago, I had no clue what a doula was. We were living in Colorado, and it was hip to be hippy, earthy, and all nat-u-ral. It seemed as if every one of our pregnant friends had a doula, so we did the research and joined the party. After the experience of having three doulas during each of our children's births, let me tell you what an incredible gift they are.

Doulas are experts in childbirth. They know how to communicate with the hospital staff, nurses, doctors, and midwives. But doulas also become experts about the parents of the soon-to-be-born baby. They spend time understanding the parents' desires for their childbirth experience. Doulas come alongside the mom-to-be and serve as an advocate for her. They are there in critical situations, when someone needs lots of support and encouragement.

Doulas are incredible in the moment, when the stakes are high and the pressure is mounting, but there's something even more valuable about them. They told Natalie stories about childbirth. True stories. Beautiful stories. Stories about births they've actually witnessed. Nat tells me it made labor way less intimidating and way more exciting when your view of childbirth isn't one of terror, but of wonder.

In much the same way, Jesus is describing the Holy Spirit. He is telling both his disciples and us that, although he is leaving, there is One who will come alongside. There is One who will be present with us at all times, especially in times of need, when the pressure is mounting and the stakes are high. And there is One who will be with us, telling us stories. True and beautiful reminders of who Jesus is. Stories that turn terror into wonder.

The Holy Spirit is our *paraclete*. Our Advocate. Our Helper. Our Encourager. Our Defender. Our Comforter. Our Counselor. The One who comes alongside and reminds us of the true and beautiful gospel of Jesus.

But let's pay attention to exactly what Jesus said: "I will ask the Father, and he will give you another advocate"—or, as *The Message* puts it, "another Friend." With the word *another*, Jesus is reminding his disciples that Jesus is their first True Friend and that he, Jesus, will be with them, and with us, by means of the Holy Spirit.

I had the privilege of attending the University of North Carolina when the legendary Dean Smith was still the basketball coach. One of Dean's many legacies at Carolina is a tradition he started in the seventies of "thanking the passer." Anytime a Tarheel player scored a basket, he turned and pointed to the person who passed him the ball. Coach Smith drilled it into players so much that if someone failed to do it, that person had to run sprints in practice.

In a similar way, the Holy Spirit's job is to point to Jesus. To remind us of Jesus. To remind us of everything Jesus ever said to us. To remind us of how Jesus taught us to live. To point to his goodness, faithfulness, and promises to us. The Holy Spirit is the most Christ-centered person we'll ever meet. The Holy Spirit is indeed the "Spirit of Christ." The incarnated Christ now sits at the right hand of the Father, but he has given us his Spirit to remain alongside us as our help, comfort, and encourager.

As Jesus speaks to his disciples about the Holy Spirit, he continues in verse 17 with these words: "The world cannot accept him, because it neither sees him nor knows him. But you know him, because he lives with you and will be in you."

The world typically believes only what it can see. It's one of the reasons we fear sharing the gospel.

But isn't that our call as the church? To make the gospel visible to the world? To point to the passer? To live lives that are flashing arrows pointing to Jesus?

We don't do this by trying harder to be "better Christians." If I wanted to sing like Adele, I could try as hard as I wanted, but I'd never be able to do it. I could take singing lessons, listen to her albums on repeat, and even dedicate my entire life to imitating her voice. But my efforts would fall short. I could hear how it was supposed to sound in my head, but the only way I could actually sing like Adele was if, somehow, she was able to come and live inside me.

The only way we can live lives fueled by the power of the Holy Spirit is not by our efforts and willpower. Just the opposite. We do this by surrendering, by laying down our own lives and fears and insecurities. Emptying ourselves. And then, through the Holy Spirit, we get the amazing gift of actually receiving the great exchange. We give up control. We give up our fears. And in return, we are gifted the very character of Jesus—his instincts, his heart, and his boldness.[2]

Becky Pippert explains it this way: "We live in a culture so saturated with self . . . that our tendency, even as Christians, is to focus on the human aspects of evangelism and not the divine. Yet it is God who takes the initiative to pursue seekers; it is his Spirit that converts; it is his gospel that saves. Evangelism is God's business from start to finish."[3]

Before we get into practical ways to actually share the gospel with our teenage friends, we must first grasp the enormous reality that this is way more about *who* than *how*. This isn't a to-do list, a puzzle, or a recipe. When we share the gospel, we do it as broken human beings filled with the Spirit of Christ.

Go and share. But do it by remembering this:

The light of Christ has actually taken up residence in your body.

The delight of the Father is on you, and he is pleased with you.

And the power and comfort of the Holy Spirit is alongside you, always.

For Parents

- How would your conversations with your kids look different if you entered into them with an awareness that the Holy Spirit was with you?

- Do you remember any time when you were keenly aware of the presence of the Holy Spirit? Have you ever shared that story with your children?

- Wrestle with this statement: The greatest gift you can give your kids is you, fully surrendered to God.

For Those in Youth Ministry

- When have you experienced the Holy Spirit inviting you to go somewhere or do something that you wouldn't normally choose to do?

- When have you experienced the comfort and power of the Holy Spirit upending your fears?

- What would you do differently in youth ministry this week if you believed that the very power of God had taken up residence in your body?

The Word of the Lord

"We have this treasure in jars of clay to show that this all-surpassing power is from God and not from us" (2 Corinthians 4:7).

A Prayer to the Spirit of Life

Holy Spirit,
In this very moment, I'm dropping down my defenses and giving you unfettered access to my heart and mind.
Make your home right here in me. Welcome to my mess.
I need wisdom. Would you counsel me?
I am distracted. Teach me to be still and listen for God's voice.
I'm hanging my head in shame. Would you gently lift my chin to gaze upon Jesus?
I've fallen flat on my face. Let me rest in the faithfulness of Christ.
I'm wallowing in rejection and discouragement. Comfort me like a nursing mother to a hungry child.
I am under attack. Defend me like a shepherd to the wolves.
I am tempted and weak. Fill my empty cup with your perfect power.
I am lonely. Would you come alongside me and make known your presence to me?
I am spiritually hungry. Fill me with the fruits of your love, joy, peace, patience, kindness, goodness, faithfulness, gentleness, and self-control.
I surrender to you. Through my broken body, would you make the gospel visible to others? Amen.

CHAPTER 9 || THE DESTINATION

At the center of the Story, there is a baby. Every Story in the Bible
whispers his name. He is like the missing piece in a puzzle—the
piece that makes all the other pieces fit together, and suddenly you
can see a beautiful picture.

—Sally Lloyd-Jones, *The Jesus Storybook Bible*

WHENEVER I leave town on a work trip, I rarely sleep well. Even if it's a desirable destination and I'm there with friends, I just can't wait to get home. But recently I took a trip that was different. I was officiating a wedding in the mountains, a few hours away. The reception ended too late to drive back home, so I stayed in a hotel. But that particular night, I slept like a baby. Even though I wasn't in my own bed, it felt like I was home. Why did it feel so different?

Because Natalie was with me. Home isn't a place, it's a person.

As we pursue kids with the gospel, it's of utmost importance that we first understand where we're going. What if Eric Palmer had found his son Luke in New York City, but didn't know how to get back home? We can't give a tour of a place we've never been.

So what's the destination? Where are we taking teenagers? Is the goal to get them to behave? To be moral? To be better people? To teach them independence? To get them into college? So they can get married and employed? Is the road we're on with them pointing to a destination of happiness and success?

How do we get them home? Home isn't a place; it's a person.

Pursuing teenagers with the gospel simply means doing whatever it takes to bring kids face-to-face with Jesus.

Jesus is the destination. Jesus is the goal. Jesus is the prize. Our family's favorite children's Bible puts it this way:

> Some people think the Bible is a book of rules, telling you what you
> should and shouldn't do. The Bible certainly does have some rules
> in it. They show you how life works best. But the Bible isn't mainly

about you and what you should be doing. It's about God and what he has done.

No, the Bible isn't a book of rules. . . . The Bible is most of all a Story. It's an adventure story about a young Hero who comes from a far country to win back his lost treasure. It's a love story about a brave Prince who leaves his palace, his throne—everything—to rescue the one he loves.

There are lots of stories in the Bible, but all the stories are telling one Big Story. The Story of how God loves his children and comes to rescue them.

It takes the whole Bible to tell this Story. And at the center of the Story, there is a baby. Every story in the Bible whispers his name. He is like the missing piece in a puzzle—the piece that makes all the other pieces fit together, and suddenly you can see a beautiful picture.[1]

*****

The gospel, the good news that we are delighted to share, is simply a person. If kids can just get a clear glimpse of who Jesus Christ truly is, they can't help but fall in love in with him.

We're not inviting kids into a behavioral modification program. We're inviting kids into a love relationship with the person of God. Love is what truly transforms us, not willpower. When we adore someone, we'll gladly drop everything to chase after them.

So, how do we fall in love with Jesus?

We start by understanding the bigger story that whispers his name. But start with your story first.

Creation

Be still for a moment. Notice your senses. See if you can hear the beat of your own heart. What do you smell? Look at the detail in your hands. Feel the breath come out of your mouth. It's unbelievable that you're alive. But you're not just a body, there's a soul in there too. You're experiencing emotion and feeling, even as you read these words.

We cannot help but acknowledge that we are not an accident. We were created on purpose, as part of a bigger story. And the Storyteller, the One who has always been and always will be, has his eyes fixed on us. Eyes of love. Like a perfect father admiring his newborn child.

The Giver of life didn't just knit together our bodies. He actually breathed his life into us. And as he did, he created us in his very image. He then gifted us the thrilling abilities to think and feel. And he sculpted us into existence with a purpose: to enjoy him, to be in relationship with him, and to worship him.

Fall

But something went wrong. The same thing we watch happen with many of our teenage friends happened with all of us. We rebelled. We tried to find our joy in other places. We turned our backs on the One who loves us most. We used the very breath he breathed into us to curse his holy name. We worshipped ourselves and the lustful desires of our flesh. And in turn, we robbed God of his glory.

God is holy and just. Even though we were his children, we became strangers and enemies to God because of our sin and rebellion. We ran away and began to worship ourselves. We became slaves to sin.

I once heard my friend David Page talking to a group of high schoolers about how God hates sin. He said, "If you have ever been lied to, you know why God hates sin. If you have ever been betrayed, you know why God hates sin. If you have ever been mocked or cursed, you know why God hates sin. If you have ever given your body away and your heart went with it, you know why God hates sin. If you have ever heard your loved ones fighting, you know why God hates sin. If you have ever been trapped by an addiction you just can't beat, you know why God hates sin."

God's heart was broken by our sin, but as a parent estranged from a child, he longed to be close again. So, he set his great rescue plan in motion.

Redemption

In his great love for us, his enemies, he sent his only son. Jesus came to earth as one of us, humbling himself to be born as a baby in a barn. Fully God. Fully man. He came as King and Servant. He lived a perfect life, always doing the will of his Father. And then, he did the unthinkable—he took on the punishment we deserved.

He himself bore our sins in his body on the cross, so that we might die to sins and live for righteousness (1 Peter 2:24).

But he was pierced for our transgressions, he was crushed for our iniquities; the punishment that brought us peace was on him, and by his wounds we are healed. We all, like sheep, have gone astray, each of us has turned to our own way; and the LORD has laid on him the iniquity of us all (Isaiah 53:5–6).

If you want to know what a judge thinks about a crime, look at the punishment he gives the criminal. If you want to know what God thinks about sin, look at the cross. When we forget how big of a deal our sin is, the cross reminds us that it cost the Son of God his very life.

The brave Prince left his palace, voluntarily took our place, and rescued the ones he loves. And on that cross, he bore our sin. But that's not all. In return, he gave us his righteousness (Romans 5:8). It was the greatest trade ever made. He paid the penalty for our rebellion, suffered the death we were due, and in exchange, gave us the right to be called children of God.

But that's not even the best part of the story. Three days later, Jesus defeated death for good. He rose from the dead and revealed that God had accepted his sacrifice on our behalf. His life, death, and resurrection are the very reason we can experience salvation. And because Jesus is still alive, we can actually know the One who achieved our salvation.

We no longer have to try and earn our way to God. There's nothing we can do to make him love us any more. There's nothing we have done that makes him love us any less. When God looks at us, he sees the righteousness of Christ (1 Corinthians 5:21).

The good news is that if we will turn from our sin, repent, and trust Christ alone for our forgiveness, we too get to experience a resurrected life. "If anyone is in Christ, the new creation has come: The old has gone, the new is here!" (2 Corinthians 5:17).

The gospel is more than us receiving forgiveness—it's that we actually get to receive *Christ*. We get to be in fellowship and deep intimacy with the One who gave himself up for us. The gospel is Jesus.

And that's why the apostle Paul was so delighted to share the gospel. Because he had encountered Christ.

That's the destination. That is the goal. To invite kids to come home. To do whatever it takes to bring them face-to-face with the person of Jesus.

For Parents

- What gospel are we preaching to our kids? Do we spend more time talking about behavior modification or about Jesus?

- What is the goal, the direction, and the destination that we are communicating to kids? Is it a college scholarship, a first-place trophy, a good report card, a starting position on the team—or an encounter with the living God?

- Have you ever sat down with your teenagers and asked them if they understand the gospel? Why not invite them to read this chapter of the book and talk with you about it?

For Those in Youth Ministry

- Do you feel confident sharing the gospel with your middle and high school friends? If not, ask to meet with someone older and wiser than you, and have this person help you understand how to share it. Use this chapter as a guide.

- Do kids regularly hear you speak of Jesus? Or do you just talk about high school drama, sports, and pop culture?

- Have you actually encountered Jesus? Have you been faced with your own sinfulness and overwhelmed by the amazing grace of the cross? Are you giving people a tour of a place you've never been?

The Word of the Lord

This passage is arguably the most concise explanation of the gospel found in Scripture:

> As for you, you were dead in your transgressions and sins, in which you used to live when you followed the ways of this world and of the ruler of the kingdom of the air, the spirit who is now at work in those who are disobedient. All of us also lived among them at one time, gratifying the cravings of our flesh and following its desires and thoughts. Like the rest, we were by nature deserving of wrath. But because of his great love for us, God, who is rich in mercy, made us alive with Christ even when we were dead in transgressions—it is by grace you have been saved. And God raised us up with Christ and seated us with him in the heavenly realms in Christ Jesus, in order that in the coming ages he might show the incomparable riches of his grace, expressed in his kindness to us in Christ Jesus. For it is by grace you have been saved, through faith—and this is not from yourselves, it is the gift of God—not by works, so that no one can boast. (Ephesians 2:1–9)

A Prayer for the Lost

Jesus,

Give _____ ever-attentive ears to hear the good news of the gospel.

Give him/her wide-awake eyes to behold the beauty of your salvation.

Give him/her a yearning mind that longs to be filled with truth and understanding.

Give him/her the monstrous faith of a mini mustard seed.

Make him/her unsatisfied with anything other than you.

Rescue him/her from apathy. Pluck my friend from the clutches of confusion and deceit.

Gently lift his/her stubborn feet from the slippery and wayward path of self-sufficiency.

Jesus, you are the only way, the only truth, and the only life. No one comes to the Father, except through you.

_____ is lost.

And you are his/her only way home.

O Christ, have mercy. Amen.

PART THREE: THE PURSUIT

The Gospels suggest that when we watch Jesus, we are watching
God love us.
—Paul Miller, *Love Walked Among Us*

The Story of Christ: The Ways Jesus Modeled a Pursuit of Prodigals

My friend Steve, a youth ministry veteran, once shared some practical things
he liked to do when leading Bible studies for teenagers. One idea stuck with
me. He assigned kids different passages in the Gospels. Their task was to read
about a specific miracle Jesus performed and answer one question: "What
did Jesus do, outside of the miracle?"

It's a fascinating exercise. By looking at the way Jesus lived, it gives us
a road map for ways we can share the gospel, through our lives, with our
teenage friends and children.

Author Eugene Peterson puts it this way:

> To follow Jesus implies that we enter into a way of life that is given
> character and shape and direction by the one who calls us. To fol-
> low Jesus means picking up rhythms and ways of doing things that
> are often unsaid but always derivative from Jesus, formed by the
> influence of Jesus. To follow Jesus means that we can't separate what
> Jesus is saying from what Jesus is doing and the way that he is doing
> it. To follow Jesus is as much, or maybe even more, about feet as it
> is about ears and eyes.[1]

Over the next several chapters, we'll walk through some of the gospel
accounts and watch how Jesus pursued others, paying attention to the different things Jesus did *outside the miracle*. By watching what Jesus does, we can
practically learn how to share the gospel with teenagers.

CHAPTER 10 || M&M'S

There is no greater agony than bearing an untold story inside you.
—Zora Neale Hurston, *Dust Tracks on a Road*

IN MARK 5, Jesus is walking curiously slow on the way to what appears to be an emergency. He's been summoned to heal a dying little girl, but during his route, he gets interrupted. In our modern-day setting, it would be similar to an ambulance driver pulling off the side of the road to have a drawn-out conversation with a homeless person.

Jesus's journey through town had turned into a parade of people all longing to get close to this teacher with the power to heal. Mixed up in the crowd was a sick woman who had been bleeding for twelve years:

> [She] had gone through a great deal at the hands of many doctors (or physicians), spending all her money in the process. She had derived no benefit from them but, on the contrary, was getting worse. This woman had heard about Jesus and came up behind him under cover of the crowd, and touched his cloak, "For if I can only touch his clothes," she said, "I shall be all right."
>
> The hemorrhage stopped immediately, and she knew in herself that she was cured of her trouble. At once Jesus knew intuitively that power had gone out of him, and he turned round in the middle of the crowd and said, "Who touched my clothes?"
>
> His disciples replied, "You can see this crowd jostling you. How can you ask, 'Who touched me?'"
>
> But he looked all round at their faces to see who had done so. Then the woman, scared and shaking all over because she knew that she was the one to whom this thing had happened, came and flung herself before him and told him the whole story. But he said to her, "Daughter, it is your faith that has healed you. Go home in peace, and be free from your trouble. (Mark 5:26–34 PHILLIPS)

Twelve years of constant bleeding stopped in a single moment. How life changing that must have been for this woman! That's a shout-it-from-the-mountaintop-I'm-healed kind of miracle. It's the one that gets all the press. But what else did Jesus do, outside of the miracle?

Mark makes certain to record what happened on that day in history. Jesus not only healed her, but took time to listen to her whole story. Can you picture the scene? Hundreds of people crowded around, all wanting a moment with the Messiah, and yet, Jesus tunes out the noise and focuses in on this one woman. Knowing Jesus, I imagine after the woman flung herself at his feet, he knelt down and sat down on the dirt alongside her, maybe even holding her hands in his. She must have been so weary, so desperate, so hopeless.

Jesus was genuinely interested in hearing her *whole* story. I wonder where she started. Did she rewind back to the beginning? Did she tell him about what life was like twelve years ago, before the sickness began? How long did they sit there and chat?

And after she had finished telling him her story, how had Jesus responded? In addition to healing her body, the Great Physician used the power of his words to restore her very soul. "He said to her, 'Daughter, it is your faith that has healed you. Go home in peace, and be free from your trouble.'"

It's the only time in all of the Gospels when we see Jesus call someone his *daughter*. And then, he calls her courageous.

Can you hear his kind voice? "My daughter, you are so brave. You had every reason to give up the fight. And yet, against all odds, you persevered. Instead of bitterness, your heart is filled with hope and faith. And that courageous faith has healed you. Be encouraged. You are one of a kind. And you are loved. Go live freely and lightly."

She likely entered the crowd anonymously, with her head hung low. I bet she left like a princess, glowing with confidence and the approval of the King.

It was twenty years ago when I took my first backpacking trip with teenagers. Our guides for the week, Jeff and Kyle, started a tradition I've been fortunate to carry on for the past two decades. At the beginning of the hike, they passed around a bag of M&M's. Each camper took a few, leaving enough so the bag could make it all the way around the circle. After they were divvied out, Jeff asked everyone to count and then report how many M&M's they took. He then shared that over the course of the week, while stopping for meals on the trail, each person would get a chance to share one *memory* or *milestone*—one *M&M*—for each M&M's taken from the bag.

Over the course of the next six days, each of the backpackers was gifted an hour to share about the memories and milestones that had shaped his life. The guides and leaders went first, and in doing so, they were able to demonstrate the power of vulnerability. Once that pattern was set, it freed others up to let their guards down and take off their masks. Part of being human is longing to be known.

I recently read my journal from last year's trip. I'd written down notes on what some of the guys had shared. Underneath my friend Sean's name, four things were written.

Sean's Memories and Milestones
- The times I've made my mom cry
- The year my dad coached my team and was proud of me
- At my eighth-grade birthday party, when only one friend showed up
- When I got hurt my junior year and couldn't play ball

What a gift it is to get a front-row seat as another person pulls the cover off his heart and hesitantly, but gratefully, shows it off—in all its mess and glory.

It continues to be one of the most significant parts of any camping trip I've experienced. I like it so much that at the beginning of each new year, we adapt a version of the M&M's sharing time in our youth ministry. Every January begins a six-week season of the church calendar called *Epiphany*. It commemorates when Jesus first appeared to the magi. In this season focused on Christ's appearing, we take turns sharing how we've seen Jesus show up in our own lives. Each week in our youth ministry, leaders or teenagers will share their testimonies, framed by a few memories and milestones that have shaped them into the people they are becoming. A couple weeks before anyone shares, I typically meet with them, hear their stories, and help them figure out the best ways to tell them.

I've had the privilege of sitting and listening to people tell their whole stories in dozens of restaurant booths all over our city:

My dad died when I was a kid. I grew up fatherless. After encountering the love of my heavenly Father, now I get to be a dad figure to so many younger guys.

I was raped when I was seventeen and never told anyone for years. Alcohol, cutting, drugs, and boys became my anesthesia. I didn't know where to turn, until I found myself in the back row of a church in my college town. An older woman at the church befriended me and took time to listen to my story. Now, I get to do the same thing for younger girls that she did for me.

My wife left me after just one year of marriage. I completely turned away from God and turned to money and worldly success to find meaning in life. But God never gave up on me. It took almost a decade of running, but ever since then, I've been in awe of the relentless grace of God.

Those are real stories, and many more are just waiting to be told.

When we get face-to-face with people—when we look one another in the eyes and pay attention, mostly in moments that catch us off guard—we get to participate in something sacred. It's the holy mystery of presence. And in those holy moments, strangers somehow become siblings. It's one of the many ways God reveals his love for us. He lifts the veil and allows us to see the *Imago Dei* in one another. Christ modeled that when sharing the gospel, a listening ear can often speak louder than words.

For Parents
Our seven-year-old daughter has recently initiated a dinnertime ritual where she asks us to each go around and answer the question of the day.

Sometimes it's a silly question, such as, "If you were in the circus, what would your act be?"

Sometimes it's more serious, such as, "When is a time you have had to be brave this week?" More times than not, our four-year-old son responds to this exercise in much the same way I would expect a teenager engaging, simply with the word *pass*. As our middle child and only boy, he is typically more reserved. But there are moments, however sparse, when he is willing to open up and let us into his world. And those moments are beautiful.

- How could you create a regular rhythm in your family where your kids have a chance to share their stories?

- Have you ever told your kids your story? Do they know what memories and milestones have shaped you? If you want to hear them share, you often have to go first.

- Realize that this isn't a fast-food meal. You can't just go through the drive-thru of your children's lives and expect them to hand you happy meals of their deepest secrets and emotions. Be patient, but always have your ears ready for when they decide it's go time.

For Those in Youth Ministry

- When is a time when someone has moved from being an acquaintance to being someone you feel deep affection for? What made that mysterious change happen?

- Do the students you lead know your story?

- If you can get them out of town and out of their comfort zones, teenagers are way more willing to take off the mask and show you what's underneath. That's one of the reasons cabin time at camp is often so powerful. Try and plan an out-of-town getaway where you can have extended time to share your stories with one another.

Dan Allender's book *To Be Told* (Colorado Springs: Waterbrook, 2006) is also a helpful resource for learning to tell your story.

The Word of the Lord

"The woman, knowing what had happened, knowing she was the one, stepped up in fear and trembling, knelt before him, and gave him the whole story. Jesus said to her, 'Daughter, you took a risk of faith, and now you're healed and whole'" (Mark 5:33–34 MSG).

A Listening Prayer

O God who listens,
I am often quick to speak at you and slow to listen to you.
Forgive me for my impatient arrogance.
You instruct me to be still and to know that you are God.
You say, "My sheep listen to my voice" (John 10:27).
And when you speak, you often do so in a whisper.
Lord, give me ears to hear you.
Give me courage to sit in the stillness of the silence.
Oh, God, I am often quick to offer my thoughts and advice.
Forgive me for my impatient arrogance.
Help me to love others well by listening patiently.
Grant me wisdom in the questions I ask and pause in the responses
I offer.
Thank you for being a God who listens to my whole story. Amen.

CHAPTER 11 || NAME

Names are the sweetest and most important sound in any language.
—Dale Carnegie, *How to Win Friends and Influence People*

JUST HOURS before Jesus sat with the bleeding woman and listened to her story, he was face-to-face with a demon-possessed man. The night before *that* was the famous evening when Jesus fell asleep during the storm. After he calmed the waves, he invited the winds to blow the sails toward the region of the Gerasenes. When the sailors hit the shore, it looked like a scene out of a horror film.

Immediately, Jesus and his disciples were ambushed by a demon-possessed man. He approached them more like a wild animal than a human being. He was naked, screaming, and bleeding from open wounds. He had broken the shackles and chains on his hands and feet. As he approached, Jesus exorcized the demons. I imagine the supernatural collision of the holiness of God with the hideous faces of the demonic realm might have been similar to the thunder sound of the storm they'd just survived.

Just as he had calmed the wind, his voice rose and commanded the evil spirits to enter a herd of wild hogs. The swine ran as if they were on fire. Their grunting, squealing, and stomping seemed even louder than the storm. Eventually, they dove from the cliff to their deaths.

Right before this, there's a short verse in Scripture that helps us understand even more of the heart of God: "Jesus asked him, 'What is your name?'" (Luke 8:30).

I wonder what it was like for the disciples to watch this going down?

"Jesus, what are you doing asking this man his name? Let's get out of here. Now!" I imagine they felt much like they did the night before in the storm. Full of fear and confusion. First, Jesus was sleeping through a hurricane, and now he was trying to get to know a madman.

But just as he called the wind and the waves by name, and they were silenced, he was about to do the same with the demons and the possessed man.

What did Jesus do outside of the miracle? He looked into the eyes of a broken man and simply asked his name. What did Jesus say to the bleeding woman? He called her *daughter*. He gave her a name.

When I first began doing youth ministry in college, my mentor handed me two books. He told me to study these two books cover to cover, to pray through them as I read, and to keep them side by side on my bedside table. The first was a worn, royal blue, felt-covered J. B. Phillips translation of the New Testament. The second was the yearbook from the high school where I would be chasing kids with the gospel.

I took his challenge seriously. As I read that blue book next to the yearbook, the Gospels came to life. As I looked at each picture of the students, teachers, and coaches at Northern Durham High School, I longed for them to hear Jesus call their names.

There were certainly some awkward moments that came out of spending hours praying through the yearbook.

Like that time in the school commons area when I yelled, "Hey Brandon! What's up, man?"

And he responded, "Um, excuse me. I don't think we've ever met," I realized that I only knew his name from the yearbook and began to feel really creepy.

There was also that time at the JV soccer practice when I asked a kid his name, even though I already knew it was Craig from reading the yearbook. He looked at me in silence. The pause grew longer.

Then, he just said, "My name is Tree."

I went with it. "Nice to meet you, Tree. I'm Drew." Over the next few years, we actually became close friends, and I still call him *Tree* to this day.

Most of the time, when someone calls us by name, it's our favorite word to hear. I remember getting the chance to meet one of my musical heroes through a friend who actually knew him. We ate a late-night dinner together afterward, but that was the end of our interaction. A year later, I was at his concert, and after the show, our eyes met while he was leaving the stage.

I was sure he wouldn't remember me, but before I knew it, he yelled across the room as if we were old friends, "Brother Drew!"

Boy, did I feel like a million bucks.

It was probably similar to how Zaccheus felt when he was camping out in a sycamore tree. His hope was to just get a glimpse of the man everyone was talking about—but to his surprise, Jesus is the one who gets a glimpse of him. Jesus looks up into the tree and calls him by name.

"Zach, come on down—let's go to your house and spend some time together."

I think if that were me, I'd have fallen right out of the tree.

"He knows my name?" Of course he did. He created him (Colossians 1:16). Before he even formed Zach in his mother's womb, he knew him (Jeremiah 1:5).

One night, in Colorado, I was in the basement of a large house speaking to a group of high schoolers about this concept: God created us, knows us, and named us. That God, the Father, calls us his children. That the name he loves to call us is *Beloved*. And that, as the Creator, he has naming rights. No matter what others have made us believe about our identity, no matter what they have nicknamed us, the Creator gets to tell us our true identity.

During the middle of my talk, my friend Nick abruptly stood and stormed up the steps. I assumed he felt sick or just had to go to the bathroom. After the talk, another leader came up front to lead a song, and I made my way upstairs to check on Nick. He had long, dark hair and always wore a black trench coat—one of those kids who never showed emotion. But when I found him, he was sitting alone at the kitchen table, his face covered in tears. I didn't have to ask what was going on; he just began yelling at me.

"You said God is my Father, and that his name for me is *Beloved*. Well, that's just bullsh*t. You want to know the truth about me? For the last seventeen years, I've had an earthly father who has told me what my name is, over and over again. Drew, you want to know what my dad's name is for me? *F*ckup*. That's the only thing he ever calls me. I'm not sure he even remembers he named me *Nick*. He just slaps me around and calls me a li'l F-up."

I just held him, and we cried together.

Names can be full of painful poison. Nineteenth-century writer William Hazlitt called a nickname "the heaviest stone the devil can throw at a man."[1] But names can also be filled with great affection.

One of my other dear friends just turned eighteen. He spent the first sixteen years of his life being shipped back and forth between different foster homes. As a toddler, his mother fell into the abyss of drug addiction, and he was left alone without a family or a home. A few years ago, he met a couple from our church and ended up moving in with them. They had a small house and already had five kids of their own, all under the age of eight, but that didn't stop them from living out the gospel.

Last year, I got the incredible privilege of being a part of his adoption ceremony. Not only did he get to become part of a family forever, but he also received a brand-new name. He announced to everyone that *Tyler*, meaning *maker of tiles*, was no more. His new name was *Gabriel*, meaning *man of God*. The morning of the ceremony, we sang a worship song that asked the question: Who makes the orphan a son and daughter? Then, we sang the answer. The King of Glory, the King above all kings.

When God made mankind, he wrote it into our very DNA that we would be namers—that names would be crucial to our identity and the way we function in the world:

> Now out of the ground the Lord God had formed every beast of the field and every bird of the heavens and brought them to the man to see what he would call them. And whatever the man called every living creature, that was its name. The man gave names to all livestock and to the birds of the heavens and to every beast of the field. (Genesis 2:19–20 ESV)

Can you picture Adam sitting in the garden of Eden coming up with names for creatures as they passed by? "You are *kangaroo*. You're an *antelope*. I'll call you a *flamingo*. I'm not going to pet you, but we'll go with *porcupine*."

When Jesus walked the earth as a man, he modeled for us how we can share his love with others—by learning names, remembering names, and even handing out nicknames. God changed Abram's name to *Abraham*, meaning *father of many nations*. Jesus called Simon Peter *the Rock* long before Dwayne Johnson was on the scene. He nicknamed James and John the *sons of thunder*. His names for people cast vision for their future.

As a kid, I was the last one of my friends to attempt the high dive at the pool. Some called me a scaredy-cat, but I used the word *cautious*. I never felt as if I was brave; I lived more into my nickname of *scaredy-cat*. When our son was born, we named him *Hutchins Brave Hill*. Most people call him *Hutch*, but I call him *Brave*. One of the reasons we wanted to name our son *Brave* was because we wanted to cast a vision over his life that he would grow into, to set him on a path of adventure. We wanted his name to serve as a reminder that the presence of the Lord was always with him, and that he never needed to live in fear.

"Son, your name is *Brave*. Go be who you are." Names determine identity, both in the present and for what will become.

As we chase after kids with the gospel, let's remember the proclamation the Lord has made over them and us. We are the ones he chases. We are *the Sought-Out*:

> "Tell Daughter Zion, 'Look! Your Savior comes! Ready to do what he said he'd do, prepared to complete what he promised.'" Zion will be called new names: Holy People, God-Redeemed, *Sought-Out*, City-Not-Forsaken. (Isaiah 62:12 MSG, emphasis added)

For Parents

- Do you have a nickname for your kids? What does it communicate about your vision for their lives? It's not too late to create one. Maybe ask them if they've ever been given nicknames they like or don't like.

- Have you ever explained to your children why you chose the birth names you did?

- Do you know the names of your children's friends? Their classmates? Their teammates? Learning the names of those close to them is a crucial step in communicating your love for your own children. Take interest in their friends, and remember their names and details about them.

For Those in Youth Ministry

Remembering names begins with prayer. Ask for the Lord's help and a spirit of humility. The less you are thinking about yourself and others' impressions of you, the easier it is to focus on them and remember names upon meeting them.

If I'm ever visiting a middle or high school with another friend in youth ministry, I ask for their help. For example, if Graham and I are going to the football game, I'll tell Graham ahead of time.

If I know a kid's name, I will say, "Hey, Scott, this is my friend Graham." If I don't know the kid's name, I'll say "Hey! This is my friend Graham." And that will be Graham's cue to ask for the kid's name.

I also keep a digital note file on my phone and write down names and descriptions of kids to help me remember. Right before I head back to the school, I look over it as a refresher and also to help me pray for kids by name.

Some people have a gift at creating nicknames, others just don't. Don't force it. If my friend Murf calls you a nickname, you can almost bet it's going to stick for the rest of your life. He's got the gift—whereas I usually strike out more times than not. I've currently settled into a rhythm of just putting the word *Brother* in front of my guy friends' names. It's not original, but it shows affection.

The Word of the Lord

"But now, this is what the LORD says—he who created you, Jacob, he who formed you, Israel: 'Do not fear, for I have redeemed you; I have summoned you by name; you are mine'" (Isaiah 43:1).

A Naming Prayer

Jesus,
Your name is above every name. And yet, you are mindful of *me*.
You are so majestic that when you placed the stars in the sky, you called them by each name. And yet, even before you formed me in the womb, you knew *me*.
You are the Good Shepherd who calls your sheep by name. You know me by name. You call me your daughter, your son. You call me redeemed.
How precious to me are your thoughts, O God. Amen.

CHAPTER 12 || GUEST

More and more, the desire grows in me simply to walk around, greet people, enter their homes, sit on their doorsteps, play ball, throw water, and be known as someone who wants to live with them.
—Henri Nouwen, *Gracias!: A Latin American Journal*

IN DECEMBER, Natalie and I each made a list of our Top 10 Most Enjoyable Moments from the previous year. My list included a few family trips and other big life events, but Nat was most surprised by one specific memory that made my top ten: Saturday afternoon bike ride and unplanned visit with the Drakes.

Nothing crazy happened that Saturday, but when I thought back over the year, it was one moment I distinctly treasured. It was a 72-degrees-and-sunny kind of day, and I felt the urge to take a spontaneous bike ride alone. After I'd pedaled a few miles down the trail, I noticed I was near the home of our friends, the Drakes. Though I'd never been inside, I'd previously driven by in my car and knew what the house looked like. I didn't call ahead, but as I knocked, I found them home and available. I wasn't in a hurry. It wasn't on my calendar. I didn't check it off my list. It was just an unplanned moment of friends being together, in a home, with no agenda.

Looking back on that afternoon, I realized it was a significant moment of transition in my relationship with the Drake family. They didn't have any time to straighten things up, but they opened the door and invited me in. They welcomed me as a guest.

In college, I went on a spring break mission trip to the Dominican Republic. As part of our team's preparation, we were asked to read the book *Gracias* by Henri Nouwen. I remember experiencing this deep peace as I read the book and then accepted Nouwen's invitation to walk more slowly into the unhurried culture of a developing country:

More and more, the desire grows in me simply to walk around, greet people, enter their homes, sit on their doorsteps, play ball, throw water, and be known as someone who wants to live with them. It is a privilege to have the time [and the freedom] to practice this simple ministry of presence. Still, it is not as simple as it seems.

My own desire to be useful, to do something significant, or to be part of some impressive project is so strong that soon my time is taken up by meetings, conferences, study groups, and workshops that prevent me from walking the streets. It is difficult not to have plans, not to organize people around an urgent cause, and not to feel that you are working directly for social progress. But I wonder more and more if the first thing shouldn't be to know people by name, to eat and drink with them, to listen to their stories and tell your own, and to let them know with words, handshakes, and hugs that you do not simply like them, but truly love them.[1]

During our week in the Dominican Republic, we were divided into pairs, to each stay with a different family in the barrio. My friend David Kernodle and I were dropped off at the one-room home of a couple who appeared to be around my grandparents' age. With two years of high school Spanish under my belt and a pocket dictionary in hand, we spent the next hour at their tiny kitchen table attempting to communicate. They seemed so interested in us. As bedtime approached, I began to wonder how the sleeping situation was going to unfold. There were four people and only one double bed.

Our new amigos insisted that David and I take their bed. I wondered if they might go and stay with friends, but after telling us *buenas noches*, they pulled a curtain across a clothesline to divide the room in two. On the other side of the curtain, this aging couple was on their knees, making sleeping pallets with blankets on the earthen floor. David and I looked at each other in disbelief. We felt unworthy of such kindness and uncomfortable being on the receiving end of such grace. That single night permanently shaped the way I viewed the power of hospitality, both as a host and as a guest.

If you read through the Gospels and look at the places Jesus interacted with people, you'll discover that only a few of those conversations actually occurred in religious settings. Jesus had a way of putting people at ease by connecting with them in familiar places. He showed up on their turf, at both their places of employment and enjoyment. Jesus became a guest in their world. He entered their homes.

In Mark 5, after Jesus listened to the bleeding woman's story, he went to the home of a religious leader named Jairus. Jairus's daughter had been sick, and now everyone presumed her to be dead. It's clear that Jesus didn't need to actually go into Jairus's home to revive his daughter. He could heal people without having to enter their houses. He could simply say the word and a miracle would happen. The very thing happened just the day before with a centurion and his sick servant (Luke 7).

But what did Jesus do outside the miracle of healing this little girl? He did what appeared to be unnecessary. He took the time to sit with people in their homes. Jesus became a guest.

*****

You can learn a lot about a teenager from the posters on their walls and the piles on the floors. In our fast-paced world of slam-packed schedules and suck-you-in smartphones, it's becoming an anomaly to spend time in one another's homes.

Going to someone's house takes much longer than sending a text message. Relationships are never an efficient use of time. It requires extra effort, can feel awkward, and is often inconvenient. And yet, Jesus chose to use much of his brief time on this earth visiting with people in their homes, as a guest.

Some time ago, I was talking with the senior pastor of our church about a book he'd read, *The Reformed Pastor* by Richard Baxter, addressing the historical practice of ministers regularly entering the homes of their parishioners. Over the next year, he decided to visit one family from our church in their home every week. The following year, our church doubled in size. Certainly, that wasn't the only contributing factor, but I'm convinced it was vital to the growth of our congregation. It allowed our pastor to hear people's stories, to dine with them, to rest with them, and to get a deeper glimpse into their private world. What better opportunity to share the goodness of the gospel than when we're sitting with people in a place where they feel safe and known?

For Parents

Going to Their "Home"

When your kids were younger, remember how they begged to have you come into their rooms and cuddle on their beds? You could barely fit on those tiny mattresses, competing with a dozen stuffed animals for leg room. But now they've entered the teenage years and might as well have *Keep Out* signs on the doors. As a parent who longs to enter their private worlds, it's difficult to navigate the change. A good place to start is just by telling them how you feel.

"[Your child's name], I know it's important for you to have your own space and I want to respect that. I also want you to know how much I long to know you deeply and to be with you. I don't know if you remember, but when you were little, we used to have a nightly tradition of us lying in your bed and reading and praying together. I know you feel too old for that now, but if you would allow me, I'd love for us to do that again. We don't have to do it every night, but how about just on Sunday nights? Would it be OK with you if we just sat on your bed together one night a week and I prayed for you? Or if we read short parts of the Bible or a devotional book together? For old times' sake?"

There will be many different reactions to an ask like that, but my guess is, if you timed it well, they just might say yes.

Being a guest is often way more uncomfortable than being a host, but it also seems to be the way of Jesus.

Inviting Them to Your "Home"

Years ago, my parents decided to refinance their mortgage and upgrade our unfinished basement. Fitted with black-light carpet straight out of a bowling alley, it affectionately became known as the *Boom-Boom Room*. My siblings and I had the privilege of making many memories there with our friends. On Tuesday nights, my dad would "reserve" the Boom-Boom Room to host his small group of teenage guys from church. He led those same guys from seventh through twelfth grade. Whenever I'd come home from college to visit on weekends, it seemed that my sister was always having people over. In addition to the lack of parking spots, I noticed another consistent pattern. While most of the kids were downstairs with the loud music and video games, there was almost always a high school gal sitting in a chair at the kitchen island, talking with my mama. My sister's friends affectionately call her *L-boogie*. My mom created a home and atmosphere that invited people to sit and share. By perfecting her sweet tea recipe and simply being available, she invited them into a safe space where they were treated as honored guests.

How do your children feel about their home? Their rooms? Could you create a space in your home to welcome and care for their friends? Ask your children to dream with you, save money with you, and work together on designing a place in your home that feels safe and inviting for teenagers.

For Those in Youth Ministry

One way I love to visit kids' homes is through the hysterical tradition of making surprise wake-up videos. I've dodged two punches and have been cussed out a handful of times, but those are honestly some of my most bonding memories with kids. The first step to actually getting in the home is to contact the kid's parents. This is sadly becoming more of a rarity in youth ministry. Twenty years ago, no one had cell phones, so to get in touch with a teenager, you *had* to call the house phone and interact with Mom and Dad. If we want to share the gospel with teenagers, it's crucial that we also build relationships with their parents.

A fun way to build on that relationship is to ask the parents to become co-conspirators in your plot to wake up their middle- or high-schooler with a video camera and a leaf blower. If you want some detailed tips on how to practically do it, check the appendix.

But visiting their homes doesn't have to be that complicated. One way I've seen it work well is by rotating host homes for your small group. If you have ten kids in your group, ask each family to host one gathering a semester. Always offer to come over early and help the family get ready to have company and be willing to stay and clean up afterward.

If you're bringing a student home from an event, tell her you'd love to see her house and her room sometime. Give her an out if that day isn't a good time, and make sure to get her parents' permission before you come in. If parents aren't home, wait for another time to visit. Be wise and don't ever be alone with a student behind closed doors.

If you get the privilege of being able to see her room, pay attention. I recently visited a friend who was involved in our youth ministry and is now a freshman in college. I sent my wife a video of a bunch of us hanging out in his dorm room. Natalie noticed that the wall by his bed was empty. We already had an old corkboard frame in the attic. After ordering some four by six pictures, we had an inexpensive, fun surprise for him when he came home for fall break.

What kind of relationship do you have with the parents of the students in your youth ministry? Have you been to their homes? What's a next step you can take toward making that happen?

The Word of the Lord

"Keep on loving one another as brothers and sisters. Do not forget to show hospitality to strangers, for by so doing some people have shown hospitality to angels without knowing it" (Hebrews 13:1–2).

A Prayer of Hospitality

God-Incarnate,
You are the ultimate Host.
This is your world, crafted with your God-sized hands, built as an offering for us.
You gave us this world.
You gave us a home.
You are the ultimate Guest.
You humbled yourself and put on flesh and made your home here, among us.
You gave us yourself.
You are our home.
In you, we live and move and have our being.
Would you give me a heart like yours so I may host others in a way that points them to you?
I surrender to you any selfishness I have regarding my home and my possessions.
They are gifts, from you and for you, and I am merely a temporary steward.
Would you give me a heart like yours so I may be a guest of others in a way that points them to you?
I surrender to you any entitlement I have regarding my relationships with others.
May I be grateful for every door you crack open, and may I enter with humility and confidence. Amen.

CHAPTER 13 || FEAST

We will feast in the house of Zion.
We will sing with our hearts restored.
"He has done great things," we will say together.
We will feast, and weep no more."[1]
—"We Will Feast" by Sandra McCracken

IT WAS truly a sight to behold. I was with some of my high school friends at summer camp in Georgia. One night after the large group gathering, we walked outside to find a huge surprise. The work crew had prepared a banquet table. For *us*. For *all* of us. All *five hundred* of us. One long table that stretched across camp. Covered with white linens and fancy dinnerware. It would soon be filled with heaping baskets of fantastic food, graciously served family style by other high schoolers who were volunteering for the month. It felt like a small taste of heaven.

Until then, I'd never eaten a meal at a table with five hundred people (unless you count the sample table on Saturdays at Costco). It was quite a celebration. We felt honored to be there, to participate in something so massive yet so personal.

Two thousand years ago, an even larger group had gathered together and were surprised by the feast set before them:

When Jesus looked up and saw a great crowd coming toward him, he said to Philip, "Where shall we buy bread for these people to eat?" He asked this only to test him, for he already had in mind what he was going to do.

Philip answered him, "It would take more than half a year's wages to buy enough bread for each one to have a bite!"

Another of his disciples, Andrew, Simon Peter's brother, spoke up, "Here is a boy with five small barley loaves and two small fish, but how far will they go among so many?"

Jesus said, "Have the people sit down." There was plenty of grass in that place, and they sat down (about five thousand men were there). Jesus then took the loaves, gave thanks, and distributed to those who were seated as much as they wanted. He did the same with the fish.

When they had all had enough to eat, he said to his disciples, "Gather the pieces that are left over. Let nothing be wasted." So they gathered them and filled twelve baskets with the pieces of the five barley loaves left over by those who had eaten. (John 6:5–13)

Five *thousand* people sat on a hillside that day. The meadow became their banqueting table. The number didn't even include women and children, so historians believe it was more likely The Feeding of the Ten Thousand. Other than the resurrection, it's the only miracle recorded in all four Gospels.

Why is it so significant? Certainly, it's mind-boggling to think about multiplying five loaves of bread and two fish into enough food to feed ten thousand people, but what did Jesus do outside the miracle? He spent time eating with people. Feasting with people. He didn't just serve appetizers. The Scriptures record that people ate until their bellies were full, until they were stuffed and satisfied. And they even had leftovers.

In Jewish culture, sharing a meal together was the ultimate sign of friendship, both in the time when Jesus walked the earth and even still today. During his short three years of ministry, Jesus shared many meals, but the people he tended to eat with were quite a motley crew. The religious leaders even used his meal companions as a point of insult against him: "The Son of Man came eating and drinking, and they say, 'Here is a glutton and a drunkard, a friend of tax collectors and sinners'" (Matthew 11:19).

As a high schooler, I remember feeling some similar emotions to the Pharisees. Active in my youth group and president of a Christian club on campus, I even had Philippians 4:13 written out in script font on the back of my green-and-yellow letter jacket. On Friday mornings, you could find me praying at the flagpole, hands joined with a few other kids wearing Christian T-shirts.

There was a college guy named Greg who would come every week and eat lunch in our school cafeteria. I heard he volunteered with another "Christian" club on campus, but I was so confused, because he never hung out with us "Christian" kids. He always sat at the tables with the partiers, potheads, and potty mouths. I was convinced he wasn't a very good Christian—so convinced, that one day, I actually wrote a letter to the area director of his organization. As a seventeen-year-old, I happily informed her that they were "sending kids to hell with their watered-down gospel." By God's providence, five years later, she became my boss.

The summer after I sent the letter, my youth pastor, Truett Williams, gave a Wednesday night talk on Luke 15. The passage begins this way:

> By this time a lot of men and women of doubtful reputation were hanging around Jesus, listening intently. The Pharisees and religion scholars were not pleased, not at all pleased. They growled, "He takes in sinners and eats meals with them, treating them like old friends." Their grumbling triggered this story. (Luke 15:1–3 MSG)

Truett went on to explain the stories Jesus told—the "lost" parables about the sheep, coin, and prodigal son. Toward the end of his sermon, he asked us who we thought Jesus would sit with if he walked into our high school cafeteria. Until then, I honestly believed he wouldn't have anything to do with the guys Greg sat with. I felt the Lord gently prying open my arrogant heart of stone like a cardiologist in surgery. In that moment, probably more than any other, I became aware that the Maker of my heart was actually rewiring my affections.

He opened my eyes to see that *I* am the lost sheep, the lost coin, and the lost son. *I* am the sinner he delighted to dine with. And now, he was inviting me to feast with those who have yet to understand his amazing grace. And to share with them the incredible news that the Jesus, the Bread of Heaven, is preparing a feast that we're all invited to attend.

So often, our feasts are for insiders only. Our homes, our church environments, our youth ministries, even the language we use, can make *outsiders* feel as if they're not welcomed at the table. Jesus's meal companions were quite a motley crew. Who are you eating with?

For Parents

When my parents were growing up, the average dinnertime was nearly ninety minutes; today, it's less than twelve. And that's during the rare occasions when families actually do eat together. Twenty percent of American meals are eaten in the car.[2] The majority of families in the United States eat an average of only one meal around a table together each week. It's not surprising, then, that the average parent spends a meager thirty-eight minutes per week in meaningful conversation with the children.[3]

In college, I studied abroad in Florence, Italy. It was quite the different dining experience from my mealtimes in the United States. I remember being bewildered at how long my host family expected me to sit at the table. Three hours was the norm. *Three hours* sitting around a table! At first, it felt like torture, especially since they didn't speak English, and I didn't speak Italian. I imagine that's how an American teenager often feels about his parents—like he just speaks a different language. Toward the end of the semester, I began to actually cherish the slower pace of dining. When eating stopped being a chore to plow through to get to the next thing, it actually became much more enjoyable. The slower I chewed, the more I tasted.

As a parent of three kids who still sit in booster seats, our mealtimes are far from peaceful. Someone typically spits something out. There's at least one spill. And to get certain foods down the hatch, it often requires turning a vegetable into an airplane. We have a rule that no one gets up until everyone's done. This is certainly more easily enforced with toddlers than teenagers; however, over a period of time, behaviors tend to adapt with expectations.

Sociologist Cody Delistraty discovered statistical proof that the loss of the table has had "quantifiable negative effects both physically and psychologically" on families and children.[4] He found the same answer to the following six questions:

1. What is the number one factor for parents raising kids who are drug-free, healthy, intelligent, kind human beings?
2. What is the number one shaper of vocabulary in younger children, even more than any other family event, including play?
3. What is the number one predictor of future academic success for elementary-age children?
4. What is one of the best safeguards against childhood obesity?
5. What is the best prescription to prevent eating disorders among adolescent girls?
6. What is the variable most associated with lower incidence of depressive and suicidal thoughts among eleven- to eighteen-year-olds?

The answer: Frequent family dinners.

One thing I've noticed about dinnertime at the Hill house is our kids tend to willingly dive deeper into the conversation when others outside of our nuclear family are sitting at the table.

I'm unaware of any meals recorded in Scripture in which Jesus actually ate with Mary, Joseph, and his biological brothers and sisters. It seems Jesus redefined the term *family meals*. His family was made up of beggars, widows, orphans, lepers, and even tax collectors.

Who is sitting at your kitchen table? Do you have any open seats?

During my first years in youth ministry, I was far away from my childhood home. Most of my meals came from a college dining hall or out of a paper bag handed to me through a window, until I met Tom and Nikki Bojanski. They had three kids, all about the same age our children currently are. It's strange to think back on all they must have been dealing with as young parents, but that didn't slow down their hospitality. Each Sunday afternoon, they graciously welcomed me into their home. They invited not only me but seven other friends I was doing youth ministry with. They opened up their laundry room. They listened to our stories. Before dinner, we all gathered around the table, held hands, and prayed. And then, we feasted. Decades later, I still remember the *Bojanski surprise rolls*. Each meal came with a basket of fresh baked bread. Hidden inside just one of the rolls was a melted Hersey kiss. You didn't know if you were the *winner* until you took a bite.

What memories are being made at your table?

For Those in Youth Ministry

It's not always convenient, but over the past decade I've tried to make it a regular practice to involve eating together at almost every youth ministry event we do. There is something spiritual about dining together. It doesn't have to be fancy or even cost much money. Below are a few practical ideas to borrow.

- My friend Laura was doing ministry in a lower-income community and got permission from the principal of the high school to start Grilled Cheese Fridays. She got day-old bread donated from the grocery store and had other friends chip in to buy cheese slices and butter. Each Friday at eleven thirty in the morning, she would bring three electric skillets and cook up delicious and free grilled cheese sandwiches for any kids who wanted one, no strings attached. It was a fun, easy, and practical way to begin building relationships with kids she might never meet otherwise.

- One of my best friends in college Ruthie McGinn started what affectionately became known as Cookie Tuesdays. She lived in a high-rise dorm with almost a thousand students, mostly freshmen. To create community, one Tuesday night, she bought a gallon of milk and a bucket of cookie dough. After a few hours in the kitchen lounge, she began knocking on doors and inviting people she'd never met to the lobby for free, hot chocolate chip cookies. By Christmas break, it had become a tradition. No longer were Tuesday nights characterized by lonely freshmen, locked up in isolation, staring at screens in their rooms. The cookies and milk had been multiplied by a heart of generosity. Hundreds of eighteen-year-olds experienced hospitality, community, and the beauty of feasting together at midnight.

- Some of my favorite youth ministry nights have been when our guys' small group dressed up all fancy, lit candles, and cooked and served the gals. We typically do this in February, around Valentine's Day, and the ladies reciprocate the following month.

- Some men from our church have a monthly rhythm of eating a Rez Meal together. It's a group of about twelve, and they take turns hosting and cooking. They always eat a multicourse meal that takes hours to prepare. During the meal, the host serves the others, and then they share about ways they've seen the Lord bring resurrection and healing to broken places in their lives.

- My friend Charlie Heritage has been volunteering in youth ministry for close to two decades. He has three kids and a full-time job, but every Friday morning you can find him at our local deep-fried breakfast spot, a southern slice of heaven called Bojangles'. He's there with a group of high school guys, reading the Bible and praying for one another. Few things bond guys together like dead birds covered in deep fried oil. They call it *Brojangles*. I think the female version should be called *The Sisterhood of the Traveling Biscuit*.

- On the last Sunday night of each month, we take a break from our regularly scheduled large group meeting and have small groups meet in homes. It takes some extra work and coordination, but it's a great chance for kids to get to know one another's families. I ask the host family to serve a meal to the small group.

- When you're feasting with kids, don't neglect the opportunity to dive into deeper conversation with them. In the Gospels, Jesus used people's hunger and thirst for food and water to point to their deeper longings. There's a list of helpful questions to ask teenagers in the appendix.

The Word of the Lord

Then I heard what sounded like a great multitude, like the roar of rushing waters and like loud peals of thunder, shouting: "Hallelujah!

For our Lord God Almighty reigns. Let us rejoice and be glad and give him glory! For the wedding of the Lamb has come, and his bride has made herself ready. Fine linen, bright and clean, was given her to wear." Then the angel said to me, "Write this: Blessed are those who are invited to the wedding supper of the Lamb!" And he added, "These are the true words of God." (Revelation 19:6–9)

A Prayer for Feasting

To be used as a prayer when gathering for a feast with friends, adapted from a prayer written by Douglas McKelvey in one of the most priceless books I own, *Every Moment Holy*:

Lord of the Feast,
This meal is an act of war. In celebrating this feast, we declare that evil and death, suffering and loss, sorrow and tears will not have the final word.
But the joy of fellowship, and the welcome and comfort of friends new and old, and the celebration of these blessings of food and drink and conversation and laughter are the true evidences of things eternal, and are the first fruits of that great glad joy that is to come and that will be unending.
So let our feast this day be joined to those sure victories secured by Christ. Let it be to us now a delight, and a glad foretaste of his eternal kingdom.
May this shared meal, and our pleasure in it, bear witness:
On the kingdom of heaven that is to come.
On the kingdom that is promised.
On the kingdom that is already, indeed, among us.
For the resurrection of all good things has already joyfully begun.
May this feast be an echo of that great supper of the Lamb, and a foreshadowing of the great celebration that awaits the children of God.
Where two or more of us are gathered, O Lord, there you have promised to be. And here we are. And so, here are you.
In the name of the Father, the Son, and the Holy Spirit, Amen.[5]

CHAPTER 14 || SHAME

He was despised and rejected by mankind, a man of suffering, and
familiar with pain. Like one from whom people hide their faces.
—Isaiah 53:3

DURING MY freshman year in college, I knew a guy named Tripp who was a
senior and was diagnosed with leukemia. The day he started chemo, he came
home to find a surprise awaiting him. His seven roommates had all gone
bald on his behalf. One of them, a junior named Jonathan, had this massive
noggin. He looked absolutely hideous with a shaved head. Over that year,
the more I got to know Jonathan, the more he became one of my heroes.
Shaving his head was just one unselfish way to say, "Tripp, I love you, and
I'm in this with you, sharing in your shame."

The second Gospel in the New Testament was written by Mark. In his
opening chapter, he jumps right in and begins describing the miracles of
Jesus. One day, while Jesus was preaching in a town called Galilee, he was approached by a man with leprosy. In those days, leprosy was fatal and thought
to be highly contagious upon contact. Therefore, lepers were required by law
to live in quarantine outside of the city. It was the ultimate mark of shame
and seclusion. As their nerve endings died, they would lose their fingers and
toes. They were covered in sores and often reeked of a violent stench. No one
wanted to be anywhere near a leper.

Most people believed sickness was a consequence of sin. If you had leprosy, you must have really made God angry. Lepers weren't allowed to enter
the temple or the synagogue. They were considered both physically and spiritually unclean.

Imagine the scene: Jesus of Nazareth preaching in the center of town.
Crowds pressed in around him, listening to the one who had been casting
demons out of people. Who was this man?

With their eyes so focused on the teacher, they wouldn't have seen the outcast creeping into their midst. What was the leper doing here? He's not allowed to be in the city.

"Don't touch me!" they screamed as they backed away. Like the water parting, a way opened for the leper to approach the healer. He came to him begging and fell on knees. "If you are willing, you can make me clean."

Mark records it this way: "Deeply moved, Jesus put out his hand, touched him, and said, 'I want to. Be clean'" (Mark 1:40–41 MSG).

An audible gasp rose in unison from the crowd. The mumbling began. "Did you see that? The teacher just touched the leper. Now he too is unclean! Why would he do that?"

Mark tells us exactly why: Jesus was *moved with compassion*. The Greek word is *sphlochna*. There's not a comparable word in the English language, but it means someone actually takes on another's suffering. That they actually feel what the other person is going through. That they enter in and take on that person's suffering.

My friend Jim Branch has been in youth ministry for about as long as I've been alive. He has oodles of stories, but a few years ago he was in the high school cafeteria with a few other Young Life leaders and witnessed something beautiful that he shared with me. Jim tells it this way:

> I overheard a commotion a few tables away and looked up to see one of the kids who came regularly to [our Young Life] club on Thursday nights. She had accidentally dumped her entire tray of food into her lap. I don't remember what they were having for lunch that day, but I do remember that it was a total mess. A tray full of food was all over her pants and she was on the verge of tears.
>
> Immediately her Young Life leader, in a moment of grace and wisdom, sprang into action. She grabbed her friend and whisked her off to the restroom as she said, "Quick, let's go change pants. You take mine and I'll wear yours."
>
> That is exactly what they did. Within minutes the teenage girl emerged from the restroom looking like nothing had ever happened, while her Young Life leader came out wearing the pants that were completely covered in mess and grime.[1]

It seems like the best way to truly understand someone—and to deeply love someone—is to walk in their shoes, to experience their hurt and chaos with them. If we want to love teenagers well, it's going to get messy.

But the reality is there are going to be circumstances our teenage friends have to endure that we can never possibly understand, no matter how much we try to walk in their shoes. We can try to identify with them and tell them similar stories that have happened to us, but it often just won't be enough. But that's OK, because there is good news—there *is* one person who knows exactly what they're experiencing.

The writer of Hebrews speaks of Jesus this way: "For we do not have a high priest who is unable to sympathize with our weaknesses, but we have one who has been tempted in every way, just as we are—yet without sin. Let us then approach God's throne of grace with confidence, so that we may receive mercy and find grace to help us in our time of need" (Hebrews 4:15). No matter what our middle and high school friends are facing, even when we can't understand, God knows just what it feels like. Jesus put on skin and dove headfirst into our mess. He can sympathize with our weaknesses. He understands everything we are going through.

Jesus was betrayed by his closest friends. His earthly father passed away when he was young. Jesus never dated or married anyone. He suffered great physical pain. Jesus was abused and taken advantage of. He got angry and upset. Jesus was homeless. He was overcome with agony, grief, and stress. He was hungry and thirsty. Hanging on the cross, he felt as if God abandoned him. Jesus lost one of his best friends. He was ridiculed and mocked. People made up lies about him. Jesus cried hard.

And even the circumstances that we've gone through that Jesus didn't specifically face, he still understands. Even though he was never blind, he felt the pain of the blind beggar on the side of the road when he touched his eyes. Although he never had to find a date for prom, he understands what it feels like to be rejected. Hear the words the prophet Isaiah used to describe Jesus:

Who would have thought GOD's saving power would look like this? The servant grew up before God—a scrawny seedling, a scrubby plant in a parched field.
There was nothing attractive about him, nothing to cause us to take a second look.
He was looked down on and passed over, a man who suffered, who knew pain firsthand.

One look at him and people turned away. We looked down on him, thought he was scum.

But the fact is, it was our pains he carried—our disfigurements, all the things wrong with us.

We thought he brought it on himself, that God was punishing him for his own failures.

But it was our sins that did that to him, that ripped and tore and crushed him—our sins!

He took the punishment, and that made us whole. Through his bruises we get healed.

We're all like sheep who've wandered off and gotten lost. We've all done our own thing, gone our own way.

And GOD has piled all our sins, everything we've done wrong, on him, on him. (Isaiah 53:1–6 MSG)

Jesus gets us. He experienced what it's like to be human. He made us human, on purpose, every single detail of our humanity. And while God—the Father, Son, and Holy Spirit—was creating us, he wired us together in a way that we too can actually feel that *sphlochna* in our bones.

A couple years ago, I was watching a video online when I felt it. Pop star Meghan Trainor, the gal who got famous by singing "All About That Bass," was a guest on *The Tonight Show* with Jimmy Fallon. She was performing one of her new songs in platform heels and took an accidental tumble as the number ended. Fallon's knee-jerk response was phenomenal. Without hesitation, he fell to the floor. He lay down right beside her, sharing in her shame. The audience went absolutely nuts. Their gasps from watching the fall had been replaced by uproarious applause.

After I watched the video clip of Ms. All About That Bass falling on her face, I couldn't help but send the link to some friends—not just so they would laugh with me at Meghan Trainor, but because there are few things more beautiful than watching others lay down their lives.

We have that same privilege to lie down on the floor with our teenage friends when they fall. We get to remind them that grace is greater than guilt. We get to point them to the One who bore all our shame on the cross. If someone were to put my secrets on the screen, I'm sure anyone reading this book would gasp just like the crowd at *The Tonight Show*. But then you'd see the God of the universe come lie down right beside me. You'd see him stripped naked and nailed to a cross. You'd watch him take the fall I deserve. And you would applaud.

For Parents

- What is something your kids have gone through that is hard for you to truly understand how they feel? How could you enter in with them?

- Do you have any old journals or letters from when you were a teenager you could read through with them? Can you recall a circumstance or conversation that was hard for you to go through?

For Those in Youth Ministry

- Who laid down his or her life for you? Who has entered into your broken places and shared in your shame?

- How do you share your own brokenness and emotions with the kids you are ministering to? Have they heard about your moments of shame and how the Lord has met you when you fell flat on your face?

The Word of the Lord

"Greater love has no one than this: to lay down one's life for one's friends" (John 15:13).

A Prayer of Exchange

O Lamb of God,

You are not a God who is unable to understand my shame.

On the cross, you wrapped yourself in my sin and, in turn, clothed me with righteousness.

You created the wood from which the cross was made.

It was a gruesome instrument of the most shameful kind of death, yet, for me, it was to be the means of life.

Let me then come with confidence to boldly approach your throne of grace.

Let me receive mercy in my time of desperate need.

Here I am. I come out of hiding.

I'm throwing off the grave clothes of my shame.

They cover the floor around me in the piles of the past.

I open your glorious wardrobe and exchange my rags with your robes of righteousness.

I am not my past. I am not what I have done.

I am not what has been done to me. I am the leper who has been made clean.

I am no longer ruled by shame.

I am ruled by a God who laid down his life for me.

O Lamb of God, you died for me. Amen.

Lamb of God,

You are not a God who is unable to understand

_____'s shame.

You bore _____'s shame and, in turn, clothed my friend with righteousness.

You made the cross, an instrument of shameful death, to be for my friend the means of life.

Let _____ then come with confidence to your throne of grace.

Let _____ then receive mercy in _____'s time of need.

Give _____ courage to come out of hiding. To throw off the grave clothes of shame. To put on your robes of righteousness.

Help _____ believe he/she is not defined by the past, not what _____ has done, nor what has been done to him/her.

Give _____ faith to believe that he/she is the leper who has been made clean.

On _____'s behalf, I intercede that your beloved would no longer be ruled by shame, but instead be ruled by a God who laid down his life on his/her behalf. Amen.

CHAPTER 15 || SKIN

A leper came to him, begging on his knees, "If you want to, you can cleanse me." Deeply moved, Jesus put out his hand, touched him, and said, "I want to. Be clean."

—Mark 1:40–41 MSG

WHEN JESUS touched the leper in Mark 1:40–42, he did more than just risk catching leprosy and sharing in the man's shame. Once more, Jesus showed us the way to love others by what he did outside of the miracle.

As the creator of skin, Jesus knew that human flesh contained nerve endings that directly connect to our brains. When those receptors are touched, they elicit all kinds of emotional responses. As a kid, a bully on my school bus loved to spit in his hand and give me "Indian sunburns" on my arms. The emotional response of pain that followed was usually accompanied by tears. On the other hand, I work with a man who is the same age as my dad and is like a surrogate grandpa to our kids. He's got that old-man strength, and the strong hands to go with it. Almost weekly in our staff meetings, I get the incredible gift of a two-minute back massage that sucks the stress right out of my shoulders.

Our culture has twisted the gift of touch and made a beautiful thing appear dirty. In a screen-saturated world, non-sexual human touch is in danger of becoming rare, if not obsolete.[1] We live in a world where we obviously have to be careful and wise, but that doesn't mean we can't redeem the gift of touch—which is as powerful today as it was when Jesus touched the leper.

A man with leprosy came to him and begged him on his knees, "If you are willing, you can make me clean." Jesus was indignant. He reached out his hand and touched the man. "I am willing," he said. "Be clean!" (Mark 1:40–41).

The Greek word used for *touched* here is *haptomai*. According to Greek scholars, it's most accurately translated *touching in a way that changes another*.[2]

Each May, for the past few years, I've had the privilege of hosting a blessing service for graduating high school seniors and their parents.[3] The students have a chance to sit in front of everyone while their parents pray a blessing over them. While the parents are speaking, they're instructed to look in their children's eyes and place their hands on their son's or daughter's shoulders. I've seen some long embraces follow those brief moments of prayer. There is power in words, but there is also power in touch.

We see a pattern all over Scripture of people placing their hands on one another as they pray for them. In Mark 10:16, Jesus took the little children in his arms and began blessing them, laying his hands on them. In Acts 19:4–6, Paul placed his hands on some disciples of Jesus, and the Holy Spirit came upon them.

There is great power in healthy, physical touch. Research has even shown that NBA teams whose players touch one another more often win more games.[4] Our skin was designed with a need to be touched. Jesus knew that. He modeled that. And he invites us to pursue one another in the same way. We share the gospel not only with our words, but also with our actions.

For Parents

My father-in-law passed away a few years ago, but when I picture him in my mind, there's a clear mental image that pops up. It's him kissing Natalie on the lips, with the sweetest, most gentle, innocent daddy-daughter kiss. Each night, when I peck my own daughters good night, I wonder if and when the day will come when they want to stop kissing their daddy on the lips. It makes me angry that our world has smeared the beauty of a kiss into something that has to be sexual. When I studied abroad in Europe, it was normal to greet even strangers with a kiss on the cheek.

Parents, I know it might feel as if your teenagers are pushing you away, but they need your healthy physical touch more than you can know. They need you to model it for them. To show them that touch doesn't have to be sexual and that touch can actually be healing.

When you pray for them at night, put your hands on their shoulders. Scratch their backs. Rub their heads. Dads, when you're on your family vacation at the beach, invite your sixteen-year-old daughter to take a walk on the sand. Ask her if it would be OK if y'all held hands. If they are getting that healthy physical touch from you, chances are they won't need to go looking elsewhere to get that need met. But if she doesn't want to hold your hand, that's OK. Just take it one step at a time. Be thankful she's even willing to go on a walk with you. Convince her she's worth chasing.

For Those in Youth Ministry

One of my favorite places to stand at any youth ministry event is the entrance door. We usually keep kids out until a crowd has built up, to build suspense. Then, when the music starts pumping, the doors open and kids pour in. What a privilege it is to stand at the door and look every kid who enters in the eye. It's also a great chance to pat kids on the shoulders, rub them on the heads, give a fist bump, and silently pray for each person who passes by.

Another tradition of touch that's been fun this year in youth ministry has been the extravagant handshake routines. It's hilarious to watch YouTube clips of professional athletes do their intricate routines with their teammates, but why leave it to the pros? We've encouraged our small groups to come up with their own secret handshakes and have even given out prizes for the most creative efforts. It's a great excuse for kids to be touched in a healthy way and helps foster an environment of belonging.[5] Kids often need to belong before they believe.

(A word of caution: Teenagers are often in a vulnerable place when it comes to relationships and physical touch. It's a heartbreaking reality, but many of them have already been taken advantage of by adults they trusted. In light of this, we must strongly err on the side of wisdom and caution when it comes to physical contact with those under our care.)

The Word of the Lord

"Jesus had compassion on them and touched their eyes. Immediately they received their sight and followed him" (Matthew 20:34).

A Prayer for Peace

> Lord,
> Make me an instrument of your peace:
> where there is hatred, let me sow love;
> where there is injury, pardon;

where there is doubt, faith;
where there is despair, hope;
where there is darkness, light;
where there is sadness, joy.
O divine Master, grant that I may not so much seek
to be consoled as to console,
to be understood as to understand,
to be loved as to love.
For it is in giving that we receive,
it is in pardoning that we are pardoned,
and it is in dying that we are born to eternal life. Amen.
(*Anonymous, although often attributed to St. Francis*)

CHAPTER 16 || YOU CAME

Communicating the message has never been a good substitue for "showing up" and embodying the message.
—Father Gregory Boyle

A FEW years ago, I was ordained as a minister. The ordination happened as part of our church's Sunday morning worship service. For the first part of the service, I sat in the front row as we sang. During the ordination liturgy, I faced the altar. After I'd taken my vow of service, Natalie placed a stole around my neck. Then, I was invited to turn around and face the congregation. I wasn't prepared for what would happen next.

Without me knowing or expecting it, for the first time that morning, I saw dozens of dear friends and family members in the crowd. Many had driven long distances. I was overwhelmed. Tears flowed so hard that all I could do was hang my head. It was one of those moments when I felt the tender embrace of my heavenly Father. It felt as if God was giving me a bear hug through his body—the church. Looking at the faces of my many brothers and sisters who had invested in my life, I could only think of two words to say: "You came!"

In John 11, right before Jesus raised Lazarus from the dead, he wept. Seeing his tears, the Jews said, "Look how deeply he loved him" (John 11:36 MSG). Can you picture Jesus standing outside the tomb of his dear friend, his arms around Mary and Martha, tears still on his face? Can you picture Lazarus coming out of the tomb, still wrapped in his grave clothes?

"Jesus, *you came!*"

Jesus could have easily raised Lazarus from the dead without even being in the same town. But outside of the miracle of the resurrection of a dead man, Jesus again modeled for us the way to live and love others, simply by showing up.

We live in a world full of broken homes and broken promises. How many teenagers have stood on a stage or a playing field and looked out in the crowd—scanning, searching, hoping that their moms or dads would be in the stands, only to be met with disappointment?

We have a great privilege to stand in the gap and show up in kids' lives. When no one else is there, we get to be a tangible expression of Christ's presence to them. We get to cheer for them when they win and weep with them when they lose.

I took a new Young Life leader out to a high school basketball game once, and he asked me if I mainly tried to go to games where I knew they would win, "since that's more fun and kids are in better moods after the game." I told him I actually prefer to be there when they lose. The crowds clear out more quickly, and there usually aren't a ton of folks waiting outside the locker room. When kids feel broken, it's as if there's a crack open in the doors of their hearts, and it tends to give a little more room for love to slip in.

ESPN ran an article a few years back about moms of NFL players. They interviewed these three-hundred-pound professional athletes and asked them questions about their mamas. One of the questions was: When you were in high school, how did your mom respond when you lost a game? I can't remember the player, but the answer he gave still makes me smile.

"She told me she feels sad for me when we lose, but that even then, she still just loves to watch me play."

That's a line I've borrowed, stored in my back pocket, and sincerely used many times with my high school friends.

"Man, I know you're disappointed with the outcome, but even in a loss, I just love to watch you play."

I love going to the away games of my middle- and high-school friend, especially for sports that don't get as much press as football. If you ever want to feel lonely, try sitting on the visitors' side of a smelly old high school gym, watching JV wrestling. It's a great way to meet those three die-hard parents who go to every match. It's also a great way to show kids you love them. That even when they thought no one would show up, you came. And by being there, we get to show them what Jesus is like.

For Parents

In high school, I jogged cross-country. Yeah, for me, it was jogging, not running. I was a back-of-the-pack kinda guy.

I told my parents, "Don't worry about taking off work early to be at the meets because it's not like I'm ever going to score points for my team." But time and time again, I remember seeing them out of my periphery and pretending to act as if they weren't even there. I bet if you could see my mile splits you'd notice quite a difference between my running speed when I knew my parents were watching. There's just something ingrained in children who want to make their parents proud. Twenty years later, I've still never told them thank you for all those times they kept showing up. Mom and Dad, if you're reading this book, I saw you on the sidelines. And it mattered. As much as I played it off, I knew you loved to watch me run. And that kept me going. And that's a big reason I'm even writing this book. Because *you came*. (But dad, I could've used a few less lectures about how I let Julie Smith beat me again.)

My guess is if you're a parent reading this book, then you're the kind of parent who's already showing up at your teenager's games, swim meets, recitals, and play practices. Don't lose heart. I know it might seem as if your kids don't care that you're there, but that just isn't true.

For Those in Youth Ministry

High school baseball games can last up to four hours. School talent shows are 88 percent painful and 12 percent awesome. Attending marching band practices qualifies you for automatic sainthood.

Showing up looks different in different seasons of life. As a college student and Young Life leader, I had the time to watch both the JV and varsity basketball games in their entirety. Now, as a husband and father, I typically just catch the last half of the JV game, hang with both teams of guys in between, and watch the first half of varsity. It's important to set boundaries and to realize you can't be present for everything—but it's also still important to show up. Below are a few practical pointers about showing up I've picked up along the way:

- Showing up starts with knowing where kids are. School cafeterias are a great place to connect. Athletic practices and games work well too. But don't forget about the kids who don't play sports. A lot of lower-income kids spend a majority of their out-of-school time just hanging in their neighborhoods and apartment complexes. Bring a basketball and just show up.
- When watching a game, remember specific plays you can bring up with your teenage friend later. They'll remember, and they'll be excited you noticed. If you have to leave a game or event early, take an action picture on your phone, and send your friend a text that you were there and sadly had to leave. Set a reminder to call later and see how the game finished up.

- Strategically position yourself before and after games where the players will see you when they walk in or walk out. If you're going to show up, it's important to let them know you're there to see them! It's sometimes awkward, but during baseball games, I like to stand beside the dugout during the half inning when the team is batting. It's a great time to chat and encourage the players.
- School talent shows are a great place to encourage kids. One year, I took my guitar and left it in the car. One kid played this really cool riff during the show. I didn't know him, but I found him afterward and asked him to teach me how to play it. We sat on the hood of my car for an hour talking. He ended up meeting Christ at camp with me three months later.
- Keep your promises. If you tell kids you're going to be at their events, show up. Too many other people have broken their trust.
- Speak life over them. Find ways to encourage their character more than their performance. Love them for who they are, not what they do. Everything else in their life is a competition (grades, sports, looks).

The Word of the Lord
"Jesus, once more deeply moved, came to the tomb" (John 11:38).

A Prayer of Presence (based on Psalm 139:7–10)

Emmanuel,
You are *God with us*. Awaken me to your presence now.
Great Defender, your presence is my shield and my fortress, an ever-present help in times of trouble.
Light of the World, your presence illuminates my path and destroys all darkness.
Prince of Peace, your presence stills my shaking; your voice calms my storms.
Almighty God, where could I possibly go to hide from your Spirit? Where could I flee from your presence?
If I ascend to heaven, you are there!
If I make my bed in the depths, you are there!
If I take the wings of the morning and dwell in the uttermost parts of the sea,
Even there your hand shall lead me, and your right hand shall hold me.
Even when I can't feel you, you are here. Amen.

CHAPTER 17 || CROWNS

Where there is no vision, the people perish.
—Proverbs 29:18 (KJV)

I HAVE terrible vision. Without my contacts or glasses, I'm legally blind. Thankfully, I have a friend named David who's a pro at helping blind people see. When I walk into his optometric practice for a checkup, he has me remove my contact lenses and sit down in a chair. He then asks me to lean forward against the machine and read the letters on the wall chart, just twelve feet away. I know they're there, but no matter how hard I squint, I can't see them. Then, he starts flipping different lenses on the refractor machine and everything eventually comes into focus; I can see what was right there in front of me all along.

When the Namer called Peter *the Rock*, Jesus was showing him a picture of his destiny. But in order for it to become clear, Peter had to see himself through the lens of Christ.

We get the chance to tell kids who they truly are, because of Christ. We get to hold crowns above their heads and let them grow into them. We get to tell them the truth about their identity, that they are sons and daughters of the King.

"You are a prince, a princess, royalty, heirs to the kingdom of heaven. This is your crown. Wear it proudly."

A family friend of ours was recently married. During the ceremony she wore her grandmother's veil. She said, as she put it on, it felt as if she was slipping into her heritage and her history. She wrote this about the occasion:

> These women that went before me were there with me. My grandmothers, my great-grandmothers, and future husband's great grandmother would all walk down the aisle with me. Their stories were a part of me, the pooling of their prayers and covering carried me to this day.[1]

Part of our role in sharing the gospel is reminding our friends of their history—reminding them that they are part of a much bigger story. God's story. But we also get to remind them of their future and point out the *Imago Dei*, the image of God, that they beautifully bear.

Mother Teresa once said her primary goal was not to better the lot of the poor, nor to alleviate the suffering of the sick. It was not even to save lives. Rather, her goal was "to recover the image of God in people."[2]

Often, when our teenage friends look in the mirror, they don't see the crown. They see the cracks. They notice their acne and double chins. They see the scars on their wrists from the razor blades that promised relief, but didn't deliver. They see rejection and failure. That's the problem with mirrors: they typically leave you either in a state of conceit or desperate defeat.

To help our friends and children see their futures, we have to encourage them to refocus by looking through the lens of Christ. C. S. Lewis offers a helpful perspective.

> Imagine yourself as a living house. God comes in to rebuild that house. At first, perhaps, you can understand what He is doing. He is getting the drains right and stopping the leaks in the roof and so on: you knew that those jobs needed doing and so you are not surprised. But presently he starts knocking the house about in a way that hurts abominably and does not seem to make sense. What on earth is He up to? The explanation is that He is building quite a different house from the one you thought of—throwing out a new wing here, putting on an extra floor there, running up towers, making courtyards. You thought you were going to be made into a decent little cottage: but He is building a palace. He intends to come and live in it Himself.[3]

My friend Andrew was at Windy Gap, a haven in the North Carolina mountains. This particular week, the camp was graced with the presence of many teenagers with disabilities. Andrew was standing outside the main meeting room when he overheard a conversation between some high school guys named Chris and Travis. Chris was completely blind, and Travis was in a wheelchair. They'd buddied up for the week. Chris pushed Travis's chair to the scenic overlook.

Travis gave the signal to stop. "That's good, man. This place is amazing!"

Chris simply responded, "Tell me all about it. Tell me everything!"

When our middle and high school friends are blind to the truth before them, we get to tell them all about it. We get to help them see who they are and who they can become. When their peers call them fat, when their coaches call them lazy, when their test scores call them dumb, we get to tell them what their Maker calls them: *chosen, beloved, mine.*

Our daughter, Honey, recently finished first grade. During the last week of school her teacher, Mrs. Anderson, made a poster for each of her students. In the middle, she wrote their names, in a cute, first-grade teacher kind of way. Mrs. Anderson then passed the fourteen poster boards around the room. She had the kids write kind words describing their classmates around each person's name. Honey wouldn't trade that poster for a million bucks.

But the words of Honey's classmates pale in comparison to the truth that the Almighty God speaks over her life. These words below are the crowns we get to hold over the heads of our children and teenage friends. These are the true and powerful words of God:

- You are my creation. I breathed life into your very body (Genesis 2:7).
- I knit you together in your mother's womb, and I made you in my very image (Genesis 1:27, Psalm 139:13).
- I know you better than anyone else ever will. I know everything about you. How many hairs are on your head, what the next word out of your mouth is going to be. Oh, how proud of you I am. You are so wonderfully made (Psalm 139:4, 14; Matthew 10:30).
- I have given you dominion over this earth. You are the caretaker I've put in charge (Genesis 1:26, 28; Psalm 8:6–8).
- I've crowned you with glory and honor. After I created everything, you were my crowning creation. I saved the best for last! (Genesis 1:26; Psalm 8:5).
- Even though you turned your back on me, I loved you so much that I gave up my only son for you (John 3:16; Romans 1:25; 3:23; 5:8; 6:23).
- Sin is no longer your master, I've freed you. All the old is gone; I've made you brand-new (Romans 6:11; 2 Corinthians 5:17; Ephesians 2:4–5).
- Although you ran away and became a stranger, I've adopted you back as my child. You're no longer an orphan; you now belong to me. Forever. And all I have belongs to you. You are now an heir of God! (John 14:18; Romans 8:16–17; 1 Corinthians 6:19; Ephesians 1:5; 1 John 3:2).
- I love getting to be your daddy (Luke 15:20–24; 1 John 3:1).
- Through Christ, I am making you perfect, and transforming you into his image (Exodus 33:18; 2 Corinthians 3:18; Hebrews 12:2).

- One day soon, you will see my face and be with me where I am (John 14:3; Revelation 22:4).
- Until then, you represent me on the earth. I have chosen you to be a light in the darkness and an ambassador for Christ (Matthew 5:14; 2 Corinthians 5:20; Ephesians 5:8; Revelation 17:14).

*****

Being a teenager is doggone hard. We can remind them of their crowns of Christ, but the next minute the world will likely knock it off their heads. It feels as if they're living in a boxing ring, constantly dodging punches. My all-time favorite movie series is the *Rocky* films. Something about the underdog fighting for his life always gets me out of my seat. A few years ago, the series continued with the movie *Creed*. In it, Adonis Creed becomes a boxer in the shadow of his late father, Apollo Creed, Rocky's former opponent and trainer.

In the climax of the movie, Adonis gets hammered with a right hook from the reigning champ, Ricky Conlan. Blood flies from his mouth and he crashes to the mat. At that moment, he lies there breathless, and the film goes silent. Conlan begins to celebrate his pending victory. Lying on the canvas, in a moment of seeming defeat, Adonis starts to see pictures in his head. Pictures of his mom, his girlfriend, even his coach Rocky Balboa, fighting for his own life. But still he remains lifeless on the mat.

Every Rocky fan recognizes what happened next. Old video footage starts to play in his mind. It's footage of his father fighting in the ring. Music builds in the background. All of a sudden, Adonis catches his breath and leaps up to finish the fight. I get chills just thinking about it.

That's such a picture of how we get to live.

In those moments when we get pummeled by our past, reminded of our faults, and showered with our sin—in those moments when our friends get their crowns knocked off their heads and can't seem to find them anywhere—we get to play the old footage. We get to remind them of their heritage. We get to show them the story of the cross. We get to live it out right in front of them. We get to lay down our lives and show them live footage of Jesus. They get to see who they truly are through the lens of Christ, reflecting off the crowns on our own heads.

For Parents

- Have your kids heard you speak vision over them? Are they convinced you believe in them? That you see Christ in them?

- Have you asked your children what their visions are for themselves? We must be careful to not impose our plans for their lives onto them. Allow God to write their stories.

- Even if they're not yet Christians, your children still bear the *Imago Dei*. They were created by God, in the image of God. Point it out in their lives. Catch them in moments of greatness. Make a big deal when they show unselfishness. When they're kind. When they reflect the light of their Maker. Speak life over them. Find ways to encourage their character more than their performance. Love them for who they are, not just what they do. Everything else in their lives is a competition. Let them hear you say, "Well done," "I'm proud of you," and "Way to go!"

Write it down. Words are powerful. When they're spoken, they vanish more quickly than when they're stained with ink. I still have a note in my Bible that my dad wrote me when I was eight years old. It simply says, *I love you, son. I'm proud of you. Dad.* That note is gold to me.

For Both Parents and Those in Youth Ministry

I was meeting with a counselor friend about a kid I mentor who's addicted to cutting. My question was: How can I help him stop? My counselor friend asked me a couple simple questions.

"Drew, what's your vision for his future? Where do you dream about him being five years from now?"

That question led me down a road of planning college visits, getting him job-shadowing experience with potential careers, introducing him to older people who've been where he is, and thinking about how his gifts could be used in the church.

What would happen if, with faith, we ask the Lord to give us a vision for the teenagers in our lives?

Do you ever talk to kids about the spiritual gifts the Lord has given them? They have so much to offer, even at a young age. Help them discover their gifts and even begin to use those now. Pastor and author J. D. Greear writes, "Whatever you're good at, do it well for the glory of God, and do it somewhere strategic for the mission of God."[4]

Another way to help teenagers understand this concept is to continue to ask good questions. If someone you know is in a bad dating relationship, instead of encouraging her to break up, and telling her what to do, just ask a question.

"Tell me about what you want your marriage to be like one day? What do you want in a future husband?" Self-discovery works way better than *should-ing*.

For Those in Youth Ministry

Every August, I like to gather our rising upperclassmen and cast a vision for them for their senior year. I show an old clip from *The Lord of the Rings*. It's a conversation between Frodo and Sam.

> Sam: "I wonder if we'll ever be put into songs or tales."
> Frodo: "What?"
> Sam: "I wonder if people will ever say, 'Let's hear about Frodo and the Ring.' And they'll say 'Yes, that's one of my favorite stories. Frodo was really courageous, wasn't he, Dad?' 'Yes, my boy, the most famousest of hobbits. And that's saying a lot.'"

Frodo: "You've left out one of the chief characters—Samwise the Brave. I want to hear more about Sam. Frodo wouldn't have got far without Sam."

Sam: "Now Mr. Frodo, you shouldn't make fun; I was being serious."

Frodo: "So was I."

I then pose the same question to the seniors: What will people say about you after you've graduated? What kind of legacy are you going to leave at this school? With your younger siblings? At your church?

Cast a vision for how they can use this year as upperclassmen to have great influence on those younger than them.

The Word of the Lord

"Blessed is the one who perseveres under trial because, having stood the test, that person will receive the crown of life that the Lord has promised to those who love him" (James 1:12).

A Prayer for Vision

Be Thou my Vision, O Lord of my heart;
Naught be all else to me, save that Thou art.
Thou my best Thought, by day or by night,
Waking or sleeping, Thy presence my light.

Be Thou my Wisdom, and Thou my true Word;
I ever with Thee and Thou with me, Lord;
Thou my great Father, I Thy true son;
Thou in me dwelling, and I with Thee one.

Riches I heed not, nor man's empty praise,
Thou mine Inheritance, now and always:
Thou and Thou only, first in my heart,
High King of Heaven, my Treasure Thou art.

High King of Heaven, my victory won,
May I reach Heaven's joys, O bright Heav'n's Sun!
Heart of my own heart, whatever befall,
Still be my Vision, O Ruler of all.[5] Amen.

CHAPTER 18 || WALK

In the middle of their talk and questions, Jesus came up and walked
along with them.
—Luke 24:16 (MSG)

AS A recent college grad in my first full-time youth ministry job, I spent a month
of the summer working at a camp in the mountains of Georgia. My job was
to head up a group of high school guys who were volunteering on the outdoor
crew, which we affectionately called the *ODC*. Wherever we were doing yard
work around camp, I remember curiously watching our camp director. He
seemed to always be walking around the property, slowly, with another person
from the camp staff right by his side. It was Wednesday of that first week when
he invited me to set down my Weed eater™ and join him for a stroll.

We walked around together for probably an hour. I remember how it
made me feel so cared for that the head honcho wanted to spend time with
me. And that he wasn't distracted, nor in a hurry.

Since then, I've had the privilege of taking quite a few walks with my
middle and high school friends. It feels quite different from the typical teenage hangout scenarios. No eating. No sports. No games. No screens. Just two
friends walking together. Sometimes in a neighborhood. Sometimes wearing
a backpack in the woods.

One day I was eating lunch with my friend Fred, a seasoned psychol-
ogist. We met because I wanted to ask his advice in regard to one of my
teenage friends who seemed to be stuck in paralyzing anxiety.

The first thing out of Fred's mouth was, "Y'all should take walks together." He began to tell me about something called *bilateral stimulation*.
He said walking is actually a medically proven therapy for anxiety because of
how it stimulates the brain.

My conversation with Fred reminded me of the year I worked at the
Dale House Project in Colorado Springs. It's a group home, sort of a halfway
house for teenagers who've been in jail and can't return home. Living in close

quarters with a couple dozen adolescents was a recipe for short fuses to often ignite. The counselor on our staff team encouraged us to handle most of the outbursts in the same way—by immediately taking a walk around the block with whoever was upset. There are few places I've encountered the presence of God like I did while stomping down Cascade Avenue, alongside a steaming seventeen-year-old.

When I think over my life about the more meaningful conversations I've had with people, it's surprising how many of them have happened during walks. The first time I told Natalie I loved her, we were on a walk. Every summer at our beach vacation, our kids know they get me, unhurried and one-on-one, for an afternoon walk down to the Ocean Isle Beach pier. Our eight-year-old will tell you it's one of her favorite moments of the year. Her dad would agree. Every Thanksgiving, my side of the family has a tradition of taking a neighborhood walk together. Even after knee-replacement surgery, my mama didn't miss it.

When I was thirteen, I took a walk I'll never forget. The Lord gently woke me up one morning at Laurel Ridge summer camp. The property was silent. The sun was about to wake up. As a constant competitor, I was pumped to take a lap around the lake and score points for my rec team, but that particular morning I could barely see my next step. The thickness of the fog made it feel as if the clouds had pitched their tents right on top of the lake. That walk was the morning I heard the voice of God calling me to a lifetime of vocational youth ministry.

It's interesting that Jesus also seemed to love taking walks. Scholars estimate that he walked more than fifteen thousand miles in his lifetime.[1] And what was the very first thing Jesus did after his resurrection? Rising from the dead was his greatest miracle ever, yet what did he do outside the miracle? He took a walk.

> That same day two of them were walking to the village Emmaus, about seven miles out of Jerusalem. They were deep in conversation, going over all these things that had happened. In the middle of their talk and questions, Jesus came up and walked along with them. (Luke 24:13–16 MSG)

From reading the Gospels, it seems as if Jesus's primary method of discipleship was walking with people. Maybe that's why backpacking trips and hiking at summer camps feel so powerful. Maybe it's not so much the view as it is the journey.

I wonder what would happen if, instead of a milkshake run or a typical talk on the couch, you invited your teenage child, or one of your high school friends, to take a walk?

Make sure to leave the phones behind. Walk slowly. Listen to your heartbeat. Pay attention to the birds. Gratefully enjoy each other's presence. And remember there is One who walks along with you.

For Parents

- When is the last time you've invited your child to go on a walk with you? What about your spouse?

- Would it be possible to start a tradition of doing a morning or evening walk with your child one day each week? Each month?

- Read Deuteronomy 6. When do you have time carved out to talk about the Lord and impress his Word onto the hearts of your children?

For Those in Youth Ministry

- Do you remember any significant walks anyone has ever taken with you?

- Do you know of some good places to take a walk in your town? If not, ask some locals who've been there longer than you have.

- Who would you like to invite on a walk this week? What fears are keeping you from doing it?

The Word of the Lord

"Love the LORD your God with all your heart and with all your soul and with all your strength. These commandments that I give you today are to be on your hearts. Impress them on your children. Talk about them when you sit at home and when you walk along the road, when you lie down and when you get up" (Deuteronomy 6:5–7).

A Walking Prayer (based on Isaiah 40)

Jesus, I want to walk with you as you walked with your Father. I want to know the intimacy of true companionship with you.

When I walk away from you, gently draw me close to your light and expose my darkness. Teach me to walk in your ways, and as I walk in them, may I find true rest. When I walk away from you, make my footsteps heavy so I am unable to run. Teach me to walk alongside you; your footsteps lead to freedom.

Jesus, I pray the same things for the teenagers in my life.
I pray that _____ would know your companionship when he/she is lonely.
I pray that when _____ walks away from you, you would draw him/her to your side.

Lord, you do not grow tired or weary of walking alongside us. Your very presence gives strength to the weary and increases the power of the weak.

Teenagers grow tired and weary, and young men and women stumble and fall; but those who hope in the Lord will renew their strength.

My prayer is that _____ would soar on wings like eagles; that _____ will run and not grow weary, that your beloved will walk and not be faint. Amen.

CHAPTER 19 || QUESTION

Speaking to people does not have the same personal intensity as listening to them. The question I put to myself is not "How many people have you spoken to about Christ this week?" but "How many people have you listened to in Christ this week?"
—Eugene H. Peterson, *The Contemplative Pastor: Returning to the Art of Spiritual Direction*

FOR YEARS in youth ministry, I've often used a cheesy icebreaker question when kids are introducing themselves in a large group. One of my go-tos has been: If you could have any superpower, what would it be? Some kids have said they wanted the ability to fly or to be invisible. A clever middle schooler wanted to be able to shoot unlimited amounts of Easy-Cheese out of his fingertips anytime he was hungry. There's always one funny guy in the high school group who makes a joke about "hot girls" and x-ray vision.

But one time, I was in a group, and one of the more thoughtful gals responded with an answer that stuck with me. She said if she could have any superpower, she'd have the ability to know the perfect question to ask during any conversation.

It's fascinating how often Jesus asked questions. If you walk through the Gospels and take careful notes, you'll find more than one hundred questions Jesus asked of those he interacted with. Look at the conversations Jesus had with people. In more than half of them, he's asking questions. Jesus didn't interrogate people; he was genuinely interested in them and curious about their thoughts and feelings. It's much the opposite of how the unbelieving world tends to view Christians.

Jesus is not a giver of advice. In the conversations recorded in the Gospels, he doesn't feed people a to-do list of spiritual tips. Instead of offering answers, he asks hard questions.

But two thousand years later as followers of Jesus, our natural tendency is to *tell* others how to live. We hand out answers like Halloween candy. Answers make us feel powerful and in control. We think questions, on the other hand, make us sound weak and uncertain. We use answers like weapons, often bullying people into belief. But Jesus shows us a better way to reach people—a way of discovery.

French writer Antoine de Saint Exupéry described the journey of discovery this way: "If you want to build a ship, don't drum up people to collect wood and don't assign them tasks and work, but rather teach them to long for the endless immensity of the sea."[1]

Questions are one of the most powerful tools we can use as we share the gospel with our adolescent children and friends. One of the defining characteristics of this transition between childhood and adulthood is that teenagers desire to seek answers to their deepest questions. Part of our role is to help them understand and formulate the questions they're seeking answers to.

But it feels easier to just tell them the answers—to shove it down their throats and try to change them. To tell them what to do and what not to do. To *should* on them. To drop the dagger of *I told you so*.

That's not the way of Jesus.

Jesus was patient with people. He allowed them space to wrestle and time to change. And even when the answers seemed obvious, he still asked the question.

In John 5, we read about another miracle Jesus performed, but once again, let's pay careful attention to what Jesus did outside of the miracle. Try and put yourself in the story. Dive into your imagination for just a moment, and visualize what it might have been like if you were actually there.

It was Passover week in Jerusalem. Every Jewish family from miles around had traveled up the mountain for the greatest celebration of the year. During the festival, hundreds of thousands of visitors would flood into the city. It was a claustrophobic person's nightmare. If you've ever been in the bathroom line during halftime of a major college football game, you can envision the crowd.

But it wasn't just people. Many of them had traveled with lambs that would soon be sold and slaughtered for the Passover meal. There were five gates used to enter the walled city, and one of them was called the Sheep Gate. Can you smell the parade of three hundred thousand sheep? The stench of the sun beating down on animal dung. This wasn't the VIP entrance. But this was the gate Jesus chose.

And next to the gate was a pool. It was believed that when God stirred the pool, the first one in the water was healed.

> Some time later, Jesus went up to Jerusalem for one of the Jewish festivals. Now there is in Jerusalem near the Sheep Gate a pool, which in Aramaic is called Bethesda and which is surrounded by five covered colonnades. Here a great number of disabled people used to lie—the blind, the lame, the paralyzed. One who was there had been an invalid for thirty-eight years. When Jesus saw him lying there and learned that he had been in this condition for a long time, he asked him, "Do you want to get well?" (John 5:1–6)

Can you imagine being there by the pool of Bethesda, eavesdropping in on this conversation between the Messiah and a man who hadn't walked in thirty-eight years?

If you overheard the interaction, you might at first assume that Jesus was mocking the man. How insensitive to even ask that question. Of course the man would love to get well, wouldn't he?

A few months ago, I was eating dinner with my friend Russ. It was six o'clock, and he'd just gotten out of bed. He's twenty-four years old and still lives like a teenager. We'd gotten together at his request, so I started the conversation with a simple question.

"What's on your mind?"

Russ looked me right in the eyes and said, "Man, I'm just tired of the way I'm living. I party or play video games all night long. I sleep all day. I've wrecked three cars. I've lost my license. My job sucks. My roommates are idiots. And I feel like I'm a disappointment to everyone around me, especially to my parents."

I responded with three more questions. "How tired are you? Tired enough that you really want to make some changes? Are you ready to give up control of your life?"

Russ looked right at the ground. "I don't know, man. I don't know."

I offered him some options and told him I'd love to help him start living life in a new direction. I haven't heard from him since.

Sometimes we get so comfortable in our routines that, even if it means getting well, we'd rather just stay right where we are. When talking to the invalid by the Sheep Gate, Jesus was asking him an honest question.

"Are you set in your ways, or would you like to know what it feels like to have legs that can walk?"

John 5:7–8 shows us how he responded: "'Sir,' the invalid replied, 'I have no one to help me into the pool when the water is stirred. While I am trying to get in, someone else goes down ahead of me.'"

He sounds a lot like many of my teenage friends. Lots of excuses. Glass half empty. Little hope of things actually ever changing.

I wonder if there were additional parts of their conversation John didn't record—or if Jesus just jumped right in with a mind-blowing display of grace and power: "Then Jesus said to him, 'Get up! Pick up your mat and walk.' At once the man was cured; he picked up his mat and walked" (John 5:8–9).

Maybe Jesus healed everyone who was there by the pool that day. Or maybe just that one. But for some reason, the disciple John recorded this conversation between a sick man and the healing Messiah. And John shows us a picture of God with skin on. A God who didn't just come to earth to cure us, but to actually interact with us. And know us.

Jesus didn't arrive shouting rebukes and commands to his subjects. He simply asked a question: "Do you want to get well?"

For Parents

I'm struck by how easy it is for relationships to move from intimate to transactional. From covenant to contract. You can probably think of a married couple you know who acts more like business partners than lovers. But their relationship didn't begin this way. You know there are wedding photos of them in a scrapbook somewhere, with pictures of them laughing and lost in each other's eyes.

You might feel the same way about your teenager. It seems like only yesterday when they would cuddle in your arms, long to be near you, and cry when you went away. Now it's just the opposite. They act as if they don't want your embrace and can't wait for you to get out of town so they can have the house to themselves. Your conversations have moved from the long stories they used to love to tell to brief requests for money and permission. Either that or long debates.

I once heard someone say that "friends ask you questions, but enemies question *you*." Do the questions you're asking your teenagers feel more like an interrogation? What is the tone of your voice? Can your kids tell you are speaking with a voice of love, and not the dreaded parenting voice of disappointment? Are the words you use with your child spoken with commanding power or gentle humility?

In Scripture, any time we're given a command, it's almost always preceded by a reminder of God's love. The indicative precedes the imperative. Take Romans 12:1–2, for example:

> Therefore, I urge you, brothers and sisters, *in view of God's mercy,* to offer your bodies as a living sacrifice, holy and pleasing to God—this is your true and proper worship. Do not conform to the pattern of this world, but be transformed by the renewing of your mind. (emphasis added)

The imperative is to offer your bodies as living sacrifices and not conform to the pattern of the world. But Paul gives this command after he's spent the first eleven chapters of Romans convincing us of God's preposterous love for us. Even in verse 1 of chapter 12, he reminds us again, "In view of God's mercy"! The next time you're in a conversation, instead of barking orders at your hormonal child, try beginning with the indicative before getting to the imperative.

Pay close attention to your interactions with your kids this week. Give yourself *plus one* for every noninterrogative question you ask your teenager, and a *minus one* for every imperative that isn't preceded with an indicative. It often takes actually stepping on a scale to motivate someone to get on a diet.

Another helpful way to use questions with your teenagers is to ask questions that make them feel like experts. Maybe you're not interested at all in playing guitar or video games, but your son spends hours every day in his room doing just that. What if you asked him to teach you how to play? Or asked him to teach you what he is learning at school? Questions give away power.

For Both Parents and Those in Youth Ministry

Asking good questions isn't a natural skill. It's learned. That's why people go through many years of schooling to be counselors. But it's a skill worth investing in. You can become a better question asker by practicing, listening, and collecting good questions. There's a list of fifty-plus thoughtful questions for teenagers in the appendix to help get you started.

It's best to ask an open-ended question that requires more than a one-word answer, but the most helpful thing to know when it comes to asking teenagers questions is how to respond following their answers. Here are three helpful phrases or questions:

- "Tell me more about that."
- "How did that make you feel?"
- Echo back answers to let them know you heard them: "Man, you've got a lot of hard stuff going on these days."

Before we even ask the teenagers questions, it's important to remember they usually have way more going on beneath the surface than we realize. A helpful exercise to do before listening or speaking to young people is to actually write out how they might be feeling. Emotionally putting yourself in their shoes will help you ask better questions.

Before a parent picks up their children from school, consider what they might have felt during the day.

- That zit on my forehead felt like a blinking sign flashing *ugly* all day long.
- The quiz scores came back, and everyone sitting around me got a higher score.

- The guy or gal I hoped would notice me didn't give me the time of day. I'll never get a date for homecoming.
- In gym class we lifted weights, and yep, I'm as weak as I thought.
- The girls sitting around me at lunch all eat whatever they want and stay skinny, but I eat yogurt and salad and still can't lose weight.
- No use trying out for the school play. It's not like I have a chance of getting a part; I always get cut.
- Everyone around me cheats. I used to try and do the right thing but it just wasn't fair, so now I cheat too—mainly because I don't want my parents to be disappointed in me. I've got to make the grades to get into college.

Consider how these feelings can help you formulate relevant questions. What if you recognized some of these things they were experiencing and simply asked, "Do you ever feel like high school is one big competition?" If they say yes, ask them, "What makes you feel that way?"

Consider their level of exhaustion. Homework, practice, college applications, expectations from friends, et cetera. What if you asked them, "Do you ever just wish the treadmill would stop and you could rest? What can I do to help the treadmill slow down?"

Before leading a Sunday morning discussion, consider what could be going on under the surface:

- Why am I even sitting in church today? What a waste of time. I can't wait until I'm out of my house and don't have to pretend anymore.
- If the people in this room knew what I did last night, they wouldn't even want me to be in this class.
- I don't know any of these people; we all go to different schools. Why do I feel more alone at church than I do anywhere else?
- The Goody Two-shoes beside me knows all the answers, but I have no clue what he's talking about. I bet his parents aren't nearly as disappointed with him as mine are with me.
- What does this story that happened thousands of years ago have to do with my life today?
- No one knows what it's like to live in my house. How can my parents even bring me to church when they fight all the time? I don't even think my dad likes my mom anymore, yet they just smile as soon as we walk in the doors. I guess that's what I'll do too.

Consider how you can formulate thoughtful questions knowing the undercurrent of what they might be feeling on a Sunday morning. "Do any of you ever feel like you have to pretend to be someone you're not when you come to church? If church is supposed to be a place where you can be honest and real, why do you think we feel like we have to fake it?"

Before telling a story to open a talk, consider the stories your teenage friends are telling themselves:

- I'm so exhausted. I went to bed at one o'clock in the morning because my teachers give us way too much homework, then I woke up six hours later to my dad yelling at me to get out of bed. Then I had to sit in classes all day long, then I had practice, and now I'm here. Got to do it all over again tomorrow.
- I wonder if my leaders would accept me if they knew how dirty I was. Not a day goes by when I don't replay over and over in my mind what my uncle did to me.
- I'm so thankful to be here. I just wish one of my leaders would notice me and invest in me. I'm hungry to learn, but I feel like the leaders give all the attention to the cool kids.
- My mom's cancer came back. How can God be real and let this happen to me?
- I think I'm addicted to sex. I look at porn every day and have already undressed every girl in this room in my mind tonight. I can't stop. And I'm not sure I even want to.
- I know we're going out to lunch afterward, and I'm going to eat whatever I want. I just hope no one notices when I make myself throw up afterward. Summer is two months away, and I've got to fit into that bikini.
- My friends talk about me behind my back, and my boyfriend cheated on me. How can I ever trust anyone again, much less trust God?
- I'm not sure why I'm here tonight, but I'm searching for something more in life, and I'm not sure where else to look.

When you're giving a talk to teenagers, it's helpful to speak some of these statements out loud. When kids hear you verbalize what they are feeling, it makes them feel known and as if they are in a safe place where it's OK to experience those thoughts.

For Those in Youth Ministry

The day before I sat down to write this chapter, I went to a wedding. During the reception, I found myself in a dozen different conversations. At the end of the night, one of my friends I'm in youth ministry with approached me with words that felt like a surgical knife.

"Hey man, I've overheard quite a few of your interactions tonight and, just keeping it real, it seems to me that you're always giving advice and telling people what to do and how to do it better. Just thought, as your friend, I should point it out to you." I'd been caught red-handed.

For some reason, many of us in youth ministry typically struggle with arrogance and telling others what to do. I don't think the key to changing that is in our willpower. It's not going to happen by merely making an effort to just ask questions and stop offering advice. Our only hope of legitimate transformation is falling more in love with the Question Asker himself.

What questions is he asking you? Take a moment and set the book down and just listen. "Do you want to get well?"

When you're leading a small group discussion either at camp, after a talk, or during a midweek Bible study, there is a strong temptation to use the discussion time to teach a lesson—and then later on, to reiterate the talk and hammer it in, to make sure they understand the concept. *Resist that temptation.* We, as the human race, learn way more from discovery than we do from lecture. Questions take more time, and they're not efficient. Ask them anyway. Questions assume a position of humility. Make the teenagers you're listening to the experts, not you. It's often through their answers that they discover they *don't* actually know the way. That's when hearts open. That's the way of Jesus.

The Word of the Lord

"What do you want me to do for you?" (Mark 10:36 Phillips).

A Prayer of Question

Father God, what questions do *you* have for *me*?

Spend some time sitting in silence and listening to the Lord. Write down any questions you hear him asking.

CHAPTER 20 || SERVE

Whoever wants to be my disciple must deny themselves and take up
their cross and follow me. For whoever wants to save their life will
lose it, but whoever loses their life for me will find it.
—Matthew 16:24–25

WHEN WE lived in Athens, Georgia, Natalie worked as a chaplain for Chick-fil-A. Her store operator, Shane Todd, was an out-of-this-world kind of boss. Between the two stores he operated, Shane had one hundred employees on his payroll. Each year, he threw an incredible Christmas party at his home and showered them with extravagant gifts. People loved working at his stores. Another friend in the business once told me Shane had a great reputation because his stores had some of the smallest employment turnover rates in the entire country. He's a Chick-fil-A legend. I don't know how much money he made, but I know he gave away tons of it. As a young youth pastor, I knew I could learn a lot from such a generous and wise businessman.

One day, I was visiting Nat at work and walked into the men's restroom. With his tie tucked into his dress shirt, there was Shane on all fours—wearing yellow rubber gloves and a big smile, scrubbing those toilets as if Jesus himself was coming over to *Eat Mor Chikin*. He could have made any of his workers do that thankless job, but he was not a boss who sat high and lofty in his office. He wasn't there to put on a show; it was just who he was. No wonder his employees loved working there.

We're naturally drawn to humility in other people and repulsed by arrogance. It's built into our DNA. But in ourselves, we often get it backward. We're attention-starved, power-hungry creatures of entitlement.

And it's not something new to this generation. Mamas have always wanted their kids to get into the best schools, get the best teachers, make the team, and win the award. Listen in on the conversation between Jesus and the mother of two of his disciples.

Then the mother of Zebedee's sons came to Jesus with her sons and, kneeling down, asked a favor of him.

"What is it you want?" he asked.

She said, "Grant that one of these two sons of mine may sit at your right and the other at your left in your kingdom." (Matthew 20:20–21)

It kind of reminds me of how a school teacher might feel when the high school sophomore gets mommy to come in and argue about his grades.

"I just don't understand why you can't round that eighty-six up to a ninety."

Jesus politely responds to her question. "Whoever wants to become great among you must be your servant, and whoever wants to be first must be your slave—just as the Son of Man did not come to be served, but to serve, and to give his life as a ransom for many" (Matthew 20:25–28).

We can shake our heads at Mrs. Zebedee, but we're often just like her. I've been married almost fifteen years and still hate having to take out the trash. The only way we're going to be transformed into servants is to become fixated on the One who came to serve us. The more we look *at* Christ, the more we'll look *like* Christ. The longer we practice the discipline, the more it becomes ingrained in who we are. We find life when we give it away.

For Parents

It's more tempting to want your kids to be great *at something,* than for them to actually be *great*. To be great means to be a servant—and it often goes unnoticed by the public eye. To be great *at something* means to get accolades for worldly success. If you asked your kids which was more important to you, what would they say?

I know you probably feel like so much of your life is already spent just laying it down for your kids. You probably feel as if they don't even notice. Keep going. Keep loving them. Keep serving them. Even when they're ungrateful.

My mom packed my lunch more than two thousand times. I probably thanked her twice. But she showed me Jesus. And it changed me without me even realizing it.

My dad built a beautiful farm table for our dining room. It was a labor of love. I think I gave him a hug and meant to write him a note, but not sure it ever got mailed. I haven't told him, but every day when I sit down for a meal, I think of him. The wood beneath my plate is a constant reminder of his sacrificial love for me.

What's one significant way you could go out of your way to lay your life down for your children in the next month?

For Those in Youth Ministry
There are tons of fun ways to show kids Christ by serving them.

- Help them with homework.
- Surprise them with a cold Gatorade after practice. Bring enough for the whole team.
- Take good pics of them at events and send them the images.
- Remember other major events in their lives, like the day they met Christ or got baptized, the day a grandmother died, or the day they got their wisdom teeth out.
- Send them real mail.
- Help them shop for prom.
- Write them letters of recommendation to use for jobs or college. Give them and their parents a copy.
- Pray for them and for specific things in their lives, and let them know when you do.

In addition to serving them, one of the most powerful ways to share the gospel with teenagers is by inviting them to actually serve alongside of you. In doing that, they get to walk in the ways of Jesus.

My friend Bill used to take high schoolers to these amazing summer camps where many of them encountered Christ. But he got frustrated trying to top the experience each year, so he started brainstorming a different method of sharing the gospel.

"What if, instead of taking kids who've already been to camp back to the same place, we go a different way? What if we make them a minority?"

Bill made phone calls to connections in the DC area, and set up a mission trip for kids who didn't even know Jesus. He took a bus full of kids to one of the poorest parts of the city. They stayed in a small house, with only two bathrooms for almost fifty people. Each day, they would do manual labor and serve the poor. They couldn't go anywhere alone because it wasn't safe. Bill introduced the suburban kids to some hard-core inner-city folks whose lives had been transformed by Christ. Those new creations powerfully shared their unfiltered stories. It was as if a shipwrecked sailor had been rescued and was telling his family back home all the exciting details. The chance for kids to actually serve others opened their hearts to the gospel in fresh ways.

How could you invite kids to serve alongside you on a regular basis? What if, instead of a playing basketball, you took kids to rake a widow's yard? What if, instead of holding your small group at your church, you met in a local nursing home and invited some residents to join you? What if, instead of breakfast Bible study, one morning you served together at the homeless shelter? What if everyone in your youth group agreed together to give up lunch each Friday for a month, then at the end of the month you pooled the money together to buy a used car for a needy family?

We find life when we give it away.

The Word of the Lord

"Do nothing out of selfish ambition or vain conceit. Rather, in humility value others above yourselves, not looking to your own interests but each of you to the interests of the others" (Philippians 2:3–4).

A Prayer for Humility (written by John Wesley)[1]

O Lamb of God, who both by Your example and precept did instruct us to be meek and humble, give me grace, throughout my whole life, in every thought, and word, and work, to imitate your meekness and humility. O mortify in me the whole body of pride. Grant me to feel that I am nothing, and have nothing, and that I deserve nothing but shame and contempt, but misery and punishment without Your mercy and grace.

Grant, O Lord, that I may look for nothing, claim nothing, and resent nothing, and that I may go through all the scenes of life, not seeking my own glory, but looking wholly unto You, and acting wholly for You.

Let me never speak any word that may tend to my own praise, unless the good of my neighbour requires it. And even then let me beware, lest to heal another, I wound my own soul. Let my ears and my heart be ever shut to the praise that cometh of people; and let me refuse to hear the voice of the charmer, charm me ever so sweetly. Give me a dread of undue applause, in whatsoever form, and from whatsoever tongue it comes.

O giver of every good and perfect gift, if at any time you please to work by my hand, teach me to discern what is my own from what is another's, and to render unto you the things that are yours. As all the good that is done on earth you do it yourself, let me ever return to you all the glory. Let me, as a pure crystal, transmit all the light you pour upon me; but never claim as my own what is your sole property. Amen.

CHAPTER 21 || FIX

Often we are not able to cure, but we are always able to care.
—Henri Nouwen, *Bread for the Journey: A
Daybook of Wisdom and Faith*

THE YEAR after Jesus healed the man by the Sheep Gate, he returned to Jerusalem for another Passover celebration. Entering the city, along with hundreds of thousands of sheep, he knew this time he would become the lamb that was led to the slaughter. And yet, even knowing his sacrificial death was only twenty-four hours away, he again modeled for us *the Jesus way* through a basin and a towel:

> Jesus knew that the Father had put all things under his power, and that he had come from God and was returning to God; so he got up from the meal, took off his outer clothing, and wrapped a towel around his waist. After that, he poured water into a basin and began to wash his disciples' feet, drying them with the towel that was wrapped around him. (John 13:3–5)

There was God in the flesh, scrubbing the feet of twelve young men. And even though one of those men, Judas, was about to betray him for a bag of silver coins, Jesus washed his betrayer's feet.

The Lamb of God didn't lecture his disciple. He didn't try to talk him out of it, even though he knew what was coming. Jesus simply loved Judas, cared for him, and cleansed his disgusting feet—the feet of a young man who would soon turn him over to be murdered.

When I worked at the Dale House Project, I encountered a lot of misguided teenagers who reminded me of Judas. One minute they would act like my best friend, and minutes later they'd lie to my face, with a smile. As hard as I tried to help them, I couldn't fix them.

The juvenile recidivism rate in Colorado was around ninety percent at the time. In my year at the project, I watched dozens of kids return to jail. I absolutely hated watching it happen. But I felt helpless to enact any change.

One morning at staff meeting, my boss, George Sheffer, spoke some words that just might be the most influential talk I've ever heard in regard to youth ministry. He talked about why we were to live life the way we did at the Dale House, with our first priority not being to change kids, but simply to love them. He then read these words from Henri Nouwen:

> Care is something other than cure. *Cure* means "change." A doctor, a lawyer, a minister, a social worker—they all want to use their professional skills to bring about changes in people's lives. They get paid for whatever kind of cure they can bring about. But cure, desirable as it may be, can easily become violent, manipulative, and even destructive if it does not grow out of care. Care is being with, crying out with, suffering with, feeling with. Care is compassion. It is claiming the truth that the other person is my brother or sister, human, mortal, vulnerable, like I am.
>
> When care is our first concern, cure can be received as a gift. Often we are not able to cure, but we are always able to care. To care is to be human.[1]

One of our residents at the house was named Vince. As a kid, he regularly got roughed up by his drunken dad. To escape the pain of his childhood, he turned to drugs, violence, and stealing cars. He bragged that he'd stolen more than a hundred vehicles. Before the age of ten, his street gang became his family. They raised him, and they owned him. But when the big hit went down, they let him take the fall, and he spent almost half his teenage years in jail. When he arrived at the Dale House, he wasn't angry; he was absent of emotion. He didn't want to get out of bed, much less get a job.

Over time, he slowly began to lower his relational walls. I even saw him smile while we danced at the seventh-inning stretch of a Rockies baseball game. We went hiking at Rocky Mountain National Park, and he laughed at me as I came down with an awful case of altitude sickness. He got his first real job at McDonald's and even started taking a class to study for his GED. After five months, when he woke up on his birthday, he had seventeen balloons in his room. That night, when he got home from flipping burgers, we threw him a surprise party with streamers, presents, and a real cake with

Happy B-day Vince on top. Nonchalantly, after the candles were blown out
and the singing was done, in almost a whisper, he said ten words that still
make my eyes sweat:
  "This is the first real birthday party I've ever had."
  A month later, Vince broke parole and was sent back to jail.
  Sadly, I've since lost touch with Vince. I don't know where he is right
now—maybe still behind bars. But my guess is, wherever he is, he still remembers that party. He still remembers being loved. And just maybe, in God's
great providence, the Lord will use those memories to draw Vince to himself.
  So often, our relationships with people become manipulative. They be-
come a contract—"I'll love you, if . . . "
  If you do this for me. If you change. If you hold up your end of the bargain.
  As we pursue teenagers, both as parents, friends, and ministers of the
gospel, we get to show them the unconditional love of Christ. We get the
privilege to love them without the responsibility of trying to fix them. That's
God's job.
  Have you seen the viral YouTube video called "It's Not about the Nail"?[2]
If you haven't, put down the book and Google it right now. It's only two
minutes, and it's hilarious. In the clip, a married couple is sitting on a couch,
and the wife is oblivious to the fact that she has a large nail embedded in her
skull. She keeps going on and on, complaining to her husband about her
headache and snagged sweaters. He tries to interrupt and point out that if she
would just remove the nail, it might help. She doesn't listen. She's not looking
for a solution to her problem; she doesn't want to be fixed. She just wants her
husband to listen to her, to be with her, and to love her in her mess.
  The reason the video is so funny is because watching it's like looking in
the mirror. I'm so quick to try to fix people that I often miss opportunities
to love them. Yesterday, in our church staff meeting, I hurt a friend. We were
discussing a scheduling problem with our Sunday morning services, and I was
convinced my solution was the best. I quickly ended any discussion with a pas-
sionate assertion of my will. I wanted to be right more than I wanted to love.
  It's a reccurring problem.
  Last Friday night, our family went out for dinner. After wait times of
more than an hour at the first three restaurants, we ended up at Ruby Tuesday.
Their croutons are like candy. We have three young kids and attempted to
save a few dollars by having them split two kids' meals. That one bad decision,
combined with an argument over the only purple crayon, led to plenty of tears,

three to-go boxes, and a quick escape from the Friday night stares. The entire drive home, I sternly lectured them about how disappointed I was with their behavior. They exited the minivan, heads hung low. Natalie made me aware that I had clearly made my point and could "give it a rest." It was not one of my prouder moments. I wanted them fixed more than I wanted them loved.

When Nat was a freshman in college, she stopped at a gas station to fill up her Honda Accord. When she picked up the nozzle, she was confused because it seemed too big to fit in her car. She was in a hurry, so she shrugged it off and held the gas gun flush with the entry point on the side of her car. Some gas spilled out, but she got enough in to get her back on the road. The car started and made it about fifty feet into the next major intersection before it completely shut down. Having no clue what to do, Natalie called her dad. She explained the situation and mentioned about the large nozzle at the gas station.

"Sweetie, did you put diesel in your car, instead of gas?"

Her stomach knotted. Although she was on a full-ride academic scholarship, in that moment, she felt quite foolish.

We didn't know each other at the time, but years later, she told me the story. The reason she even told me was because she wanted me to know how her daddy responded.

"It's OK, honey, don't you worry at all; we'll get this worked out. Tell me your cross streets, and I'm going to call AAA. I'll be there in an hour. I love you."

In a moment of failure, instead of a lecture, my future father-in-law offered grace. And I'm so grateful he did. I've never met a more grace-filled person than my precious wife, and I have her daddy to thank for that.

As we interact with teenagers, it's extremely tempting to offer advice and point out their nails. The more time I spend with them, the more I think my father-in-law hit the nail on the head.

As young adults, authors Christian and Amy Piatt wrote the following words to older generations:

> We long for your wisdom and guidance. We seek to learn from your struggles, successes, and failures. . . . The trouble is that sometimes we don't know how to ask for your help because we don't know what we need. We don't know if we can trust you, and we don't know if you really want to know us.

We need help getting over the notion that all you want to do is tell us what we are doing wrong.

If you try to fix us, we will resent you. If you share with us about how you found hope, we will appreciate you.

We know a phony when we see one. We also know when you are being real. . . . We crave authenticity.

We need help finding our way to your door, so you'll probably need to come to us first.[3]

What does it look like for us to come alongside the teenagers in our lives with no agenda other than love? Many of them feel like wounded animals, beaten up by the world, and they're not about to come out of hiding and risk being kicked again. We're going to have to come to them first.

For Parents

One of my favorite musicians tells a story about a significant moment of healing in his life—in the back lounge of a tour bus.

I had just poured out my broken heart to my friend, Andy, when I recognized in the silence that fell between us that I was bracing myself for what he would say next. Would he try to fix me? Correct me? Would he reject my pain by offering answers?

After a moment Andy said, "Jason, I want you to stand up with me. Here's what we're going to do. I'm going to hug you, and you need to let me hold you for at least two minutes. And I'm going to time it," he said as he took off his watch, "so you're not going anywhere."

I'm not afraid of male bonding, but two minutes is a long time to hug anyone, let alone in the back lounge of a tour bus. I laughed nervously at first because I felt awkward. But then I found myself crying, and not long after that I started *ugly* crying. And then, as the last bit of strength I had been clinging to gave itself up, I felt like I sort of went limp and mostly just hung there, held up in the arms of my friend. He didn't ask me to be okay. He didn't offer answers. He just offered himself.

Pain is holy, and in the presence of holiness it's often best to keep quiet. No words passed between us, but what Andy was saying, and what God was saying through him, was clear: "You are loved. You are not alone."[4]

In parenting, timing is everything. In the heat of the moment, how you respond will determine the type relationship you have with your son and daughter.

When she has her first fender bender.
When you catch your son looking at porn.
When you overhear your daughter making herself throw up.
When the cops call you and you find out your kid isn't the angel you thought.

How you respond in those moments will shape how your child views his or her own identity. In a moment of failure, will you remind your kids that they are wrong or that they are loved? Will you lecture them or hold them?

Sure, there will come a time when a hard conversation is needed, but in the moment, remind them of the grace of the cross. Tell them with your presence that they are loved and not alone.

For Those in Youth Ministry

- Are kids convinced you care about them more than you want to cure them?

- Do they feel condemned by you or loved by you?

- When they're pouring out their hearts to you, do you respond with advice, or with a nod?

The Word of the Lord

"He went to [the injured man] and bandaged his wounds, pouring on oil and wine. Then he put the man on his own donkey, brought him to an inn and took care of him" (Luke 10:34).

A Prayer for Care

Tender Father,
On behalf of _____, I cast your beloved's cares on you because you care for your child.
Would you comfort _____'s heart through the tender compassion of your Holy Spirit?
Meet your beloved in his or her weakness. Tend to his or her wounds. Bind up the broken places.
Hold _____ tightly. Hold _____ gently. Your embrace is constant comfort. Even when your beloved feels as if he or she has betrayed you, may _____ know that you still long to wash his or her feet. Amen.

CHAPTER 22 || GRACE

Yet, though sin is shown to be wide and deep, thank God his grace is
wider and deeper still!
—Romans 5:20 (PHILLIPS)

MY FAVORITE thing to watch on YouTube is fail videos. It's the modern-day version of how I spent many elementary school Friday nights, watching Bob Saget and *America's Funniest Home Videos*.

Natalie's not much for social media, but on the rare occasion she does post something, it's usually a hilarious Pinterest fail with the hashtag #NailedIt! I especially enjoyed the time she and the kids put marshmallows in crescent rolls to make "resurrection rolls" for Easter. They came out looking more as if Jesus had used dynamite to explode the door off the tomb.

Something about watching other people fail makes us feel better about ourselves. And for some reason, we're often hardest on those closest to us. Deep within our sinful nature is that sickening desire to know we were right and they were wrong. As we say, "I told you so," we proudly take a step up our ladder of success and rejoice as those we love get pushed down a rung.

Jesus handled failure a little differently.

One morning at dawn, Jesus appeared in the temple courts of Jerusalem. He was teaching a crowd of people when all of a sudden, he was interrupted. The religious leaders of the day, the Pharisees, didn't like the attention everyone was giving Jesus, so they came up with a scheme to trap him. They brought to him a woman who'd been *caught in* adultery. I imagine they didn't give her time to get dressed. The morality police dragged her like a rag doll through the city streets, only a bed sheet covering her shame. Following their parade, they threw her at the feet of Jesus.

"'Teacher, . . . in the Law Moses commanded us to stone such women. Now what do you say?'" (John 8:4–5).

It was true. In the Torah, the Scriptures commanded the death of adulterers. God takes the marriage covenant very seriously. The Pharisees knew Jesus, put in this situation, would have only two options. He could demand justice and order her execution. Or he could let her off the hook and go directly against the Law. They were sure they had him trapped.

But what did Jesus do? John 8:6 records that "Jesus bent down and started to write on the ground with his finger."

What on earth was he doing? Was he stumped and trying to figure out a game plan? Was he stalling?

As he started to write in the sand, every accusing eye in the temple courts became fixated on his words. As they tried to figure out what he was writing, their attention was drawn away from the woman who'd been shaking in shame.

The Scriptures tell us, "When they kept on questioning him, he straightened up" (John 8:7). Like a big brother standing up for his little sister, I imagine Jesus getting off his knees and standing up taller than he'd ever stood before, right in front of the humiliated woman. She finally peeked out from behind the hair that had been covering her face.

And then Jesus said those famous words: "*Let any one of you who is without sin be the first to throw a stone.*" (John 8:7).

He then stooped down to write on the ground for a second time. I wonder if this time he started writing people's names with a list of their sins. Can you imagine being a religious leader and watching Jesus write your name with something wrong you did the day before underneath it?

Maybe that wasn't exactly what Jesus wrote, but something happened after he asked that question. Everyone who had picked up a rock, and was ready to relay judgment, started to experience conviction. Stones began dropping like a hailstorm. The once-busy temple courts gradually cleared out, and eventually, only Jesus and the woman were left. Then, Jesus asked two more questions:

"Where are they? Has no one condemned you?"

"No one, sir," she said.

"Then neither do I condemn you," Jesus declared. "Go now and leave your life of sin." (John 8:10–11)

This didn't just happen in this one instance. Everywhere Jesus went he trumped sin with grace. He didn't see Zacchaeus up in that tree and call out his sin.

"Hey, everybody, look at that traitor and thief!" He didn't wash everyone's feet except Judas's. He didn't ignore people who cussed, did drugs, and weren't religious. In fact, not once in the Gospels did Jesus condemn a pagan. The only people he condemned were the rigid, religious people who were more concerned about their appearance of piety.

It's so opposite of the way we live. But it's the exact way we were designed to live. And when we see it, our hearts light up. It happened the first time we encountered Christ ourselves. We were blown away by the fact that God repaid our sin with his grace.

If you've ever read or watched Victor Hugo's *Les Misérables*, you've likely seen yourself in the mirror of Jean Valjean. An ex-convict, he was finally released after nineteen years of hard labor in prison. Wandering the streets, with nowhere to go, Valjean was finally taken in by a kind old bishop and his wife. During the middle of the night, in a thoughtless act, he steals the bishop's silver and knocks out the old man on his way out the door. The next morning, he gets caught, and the authorities bring him back to the bishop's house in handcuffs to return the silver.

In an absurd act of grace, the bishop tells the officers he actually gave the silver to Jean Valjean, and he's thankful they brought him back, because he forgot to take the silver candlesticks. The officers are stunned, and so is their prisoner. They release him and leave him alone with the bishop. As the man of God looks deeply in Jean Valjean's eyes, he hands him the candlesticks.

"Now don't forget it, don't you ever forget it. You've promised to become a new man."

Valjean asks the bishop, "Now why are you doing this?"

The bishop responds, "Jean Valjean, my brother, you no longer belong to evil. With this silver, I've bought your soul. I've ransomed you from fear and hatred, and now I give you back to God." From that moment forward, his life was never the same.

I wonder whatever happened to the woman caught in adultery. I can only imagine how her life was radically changed by the grace Jesus showed her. I wonder if, a year later, she was still there in the city the day Christ was crucified.

Under the law, the penalty for her offense of adultery was execution by stoning. When a Roman citizen was convicted of a crime, they were thrown into prison. A certificate of debt, listing all their crimes, was nailed to the door of their cell. Anyone who passed by could read a list of their punishable offenses. After the prisoner had served the sentence, the indictment was removed from the door. Upon his or her release, the judge would sign the indictment, and write across it the word *tetelestai*. The prisoner would then forever carry that document as proof that the sentence had been served, the debt had been paid, and that now, he or she was truly free.[1]

On the cross, just before Jesus breathed his last, he cried out that very same word: *Tetelestai*. It is finished!

My debt. Your debt. The debt of the adulterous woman. All *paid in full* by the perfect sacrifice of the Son of God. Jesus took that certificate of debt and completely obliterated it. "He paid the very last cent of the wages of our sin."[2]

Just like the adulterous woman, we are no longer condemned. It's unbelievable, but it's true.

Only when we grasp the grace that has been showed to us will we be able to show that grace to others.

When we realize we're the ones who have stolen the silver—that's when getting the candlesticks spring-loads us to share the gospel of undeserved love. That's what makes it possible to show grace:

- When your sweet baby girl, who could do no wrong, turns fifteen and sneaks out of the house to go to her first party
- When the senior guy on your summer mission trip takes advantage of a freshmen girl whose parents trusted you to protect her
- When the high school guy you've been chasing for years won't return your calls or texts
- When your middle-school daughter just uses you as an ATM and a taxi driver
- When you find out a kid in your youth group has been posting lies about you on social media
- When a gal you absolutely love throws her faith out the window and trades it for one night with a guy
- When another parent tells you the rumors they overheard about your kid and you feel as if you've been tricked by a child you thought you could trust
- When a kid you've been investing in steals from you
- When you give your heart away to a teenager and it gets stomped on by lies, deceit, and broken trust

How do we respond in those moments? Those scenarios are all real. They're ones I've personally experienced. They're awfully painful. And my guess is you probably have a long list of your own.

Paul writes in Romans 5:20, "Where sin increased, grace increased all the more." The PHILLIPS translation puts it this way: "Yet, though sin is shown to be wide and deep, thank God his grace is wider and deeper still!"

God's grace outruns our evil deeds. His ability to find us is greater than our ability to get lost.

For Parents
Our friends John and Laura are unbelievable parents. They've raised a quiver full of kids in a Christ-centered home. A decade ago, life seemed like a dream, but then their oldest daughter ran away—not physically, but spiritually. It's as if she became a different person overnight. Everything she'd ever been taught was thrown out the window. She moved to a far-off country and turned her heart away from her family. John's and Laura's hearts were broken. A few years ago, their daughter miraculously came home—not just physically, but also spiritually. Last year, she was married in their front yard. As a gift on her wedding day, John and Laura gave her two silver candlesticks.

- Does your home smell like grace? Do your kids know they can't outrun your love? Do you repay evil with good?

- What would happen if the next time your child broke a rule, or broke your heart, you responded with extravagant grace? Not just letting them off the hook, but showering them with undeserved love.

For Those in Youth Ministry
When I worked at the Dale House and a kid broke the rules, consequences were clearly laid out ahead of time. If they broke curfew, they knew to expect they'd be scrubbing floors and baseboards with a toothbrush. One of my

most (and least) favorite parts of working at the project was that staff were asked to experience all consequences alongside the residents. If I handed out an order, it meant I was doing it too. Many late nights were spent on hands and knees right beside my teenage friends.

One summer, while working at a summer camp, the speaker had a stroke of brilliance and came up with a beautiful way to demonstrate this idea of getting what you don't deserve. Before camp started, he asked someone to donate money to cover the cost of ice cream for all the campers. On Wednesday night, he spoke about the cross, and God's extravagant grace. Later that evening, after cabin time, the snack shack opened. Usually, ice cream was three dollars a scoop. But on this particular evening, Big Scoop Night, kids could get a triple scoop for only a quarter. I still remember seeing kids' faces light up when they saw how tall their ice cream cones were.

"This is only a quarter?"

Word quickly spread, and the entire camp staff built some solid forearm muscles scooping for four hundred surprised teenagers. A small thing. But just another way to show kids a picture of undeserved grace.

The Word of the Lord
"Love covers over a multitude of sins" (1 Peter 4:8).

A Prayer for Grace

> Merciful Lord,
> I need your grace.
> I need your grace to even pray this prayer.
> I need your grace to love myself.
> I need your grace to love others.
> I need your grace to even love you.
> I need your grace.
> I need your grace.
> I need your grace. Amen.

CHAPTER 23 || WAR

Prayer isn't preparation for the battle. Prayer is the battle.
- Oswald Chambers

IT WAS near the end of the first semester of college, and it seemed as if everyone was making big plans for Christmas break. I heard different groups talking about planning trips to the Florida Keys and the Bahamas. Maybe it was for fear of being left out, but I decided that I needed to come up with my own answer in case someone asked what I was doing. In an InterVarsity meeting, I heard about a massive mission conference being held in Illinois, called Urbana. Without knowing anyone else going, I mailed in my check and registration form, and bought a bus ticket.

Upon arrival, I met my two roommates. Both were from China and neither spoke English. I also realized it snowed more in Illinois than North Carolina. That week was colder than my teenage showers, after my dad cut off the hot water heater because I'd exceeded my ten-minute limit.

"This is just great. My friends are in the Keys working on their tans. I'm freezing. I know no one. And I can't even communicate with my roommates. What am I doing here?"

The Lord knew exactly what I was doing there. In my discomfort and loneliness, he brought me to a place of desperate dependence upon him. Standing alone, among fifteen thousand other college students, I experienced the freedom of a child. For literally the first time ever, I raised my hands in worship. I sang as if I was wearing headphones and didn't care what anyone thought of me. I eagerly listened to the speakers and to the Holy Spirit.

One memorable night, a man walked on stage to speak. I can't recall his name or face, but I can clearly remember the power in his words. It was as if God was holding my heart is his hands as the man spoke. Directly below the podium was a woman. She was out of the speaker's sight, due to the height of the stage, but she stood below with her arms raised in prayer.

Somewhere in the middle of his talk, the speaker started to lose his voice. At first, it sounded as if he needed a drink of water, but then it became too much of a whisper to even hear. I noticed the praying woman below him was no longer holding up her arms. It appeared she had become too tired.

What I saw next didn't fit in the safe and sensible box I'd been keeping my religion in. Two other people walked up to the woman and lifted her arms. At that exact same moment her arms were raised, the speaker's voice returned. I get chills even now as I write about it.

I tried to rationalize it. Maybe it was all staged? The people sitting beside me didn't even notice. I pointed down to the praying lady and explained what I saw. For the remainder of the talk, people rotated in and out, holding up the arms of the woman. It was like watching our kids be born. It's one of those moments where there's no doubt in my mind I'd just witnessed a miracle.

Something similar happened in Exodus 17 during Israel's battle with the Amalekites. While Joshua and his army went down to fight, Moses took Aaron and Hur to the top of a hill overlooking the battle.

> As long as Moses held up his hands, the Israelites were win-
> ning, but whenever he lowered his hands, the Amalekites were win-
> ning. When Moses' hands grew tired, they took a stone and put it
> under him and he sat on it. Aaron and Hur held his hands up—one
> on one side, one on the other—so that his hands remained steady
> till sunset. So Joshua overcame the Amalekite army with the sword.
>
> Then the LORD said to Moses, "Write this on a scroll as some-
> thing to be remembered and make sure that Joshua hears it." (Exodus
> 17:11–14)

Richard Foster had the following observation about this event:

> In the military annals Joshua was the commander who won the vic-
> tory that day. He was the person up front and in the thick of the
> conflict. But you and I know the rest of the story. Back behind the
> scenes the battle of intercession was won by Moses and Aaron and
> Hur. Each role was essential for victory. Joshua was needed to lead the
> charge. Moses was needed to intercede on behalf of the children of
> Israel. Aaron and Hur were needed to assist Moses as he grew weary.[1]

Chasing after teenagers feels a lot like war. If we're fighting for their souls, the most effective tool we have is the power of prayer. Prayer isn't just preparation for the battle—prayer *is* the war.

Jesus understood and modeled this. If there was anyone who didn't need to pray, wouldn't you think it would be God himself? But over and over again in the Gospels, we see Jesus on his knees, interceding for those he loves. The entire chapter of John 17 is a record of Jesus praying for his disciples. When you read the words of Jesus's prayer, pay careful attention to how he prayed. Even though he was a grown man, his prayer is spoken with the voice of a child. He tells his daddy the desires of his heart and prays expectantly, believing his Father is listening.

It's the very same posture when he teaches the disciples how to pray. He could have taught them to begin with "Almighty Maker of the universe," but in the one place recorded in all of Scripture, when Jesus is asked to teach us how to pray, he begins with two words: *Our Father.*

The very words disarm us. They signal our dependence as children. They remind us that prayer isn't a performance or a magic formula—it's actually a personal interaction with a living God.

It also reminds us that our Father is the God of all angel armies. He's the One who silences the storms. He's the miracle worker, not us.

So often we take matters back into our own hands. We try and fight the war through sheer willpower. If I can just be cool enough, or funny enough, or go to enough of their games, this kid will meet Jesus. Maybe if we switch churches again and go to one with a better youth group, my teenager will follow Christ. If only I was smarter and could answer their hard questions about Christianity, maybe then they would understand Jesus, but I just feel so weak.

The only way to win the war is through surrender.

For Parents

Spend some time reading Jesus's prayer in John 17. Notice what Jesus prayed for:

- He acknowledged they were given to him by God.
- He asked for their protection.
- He prayed for their unity.
- He asked for them to have joy.
- He prayed they would be holy.
- He asked that they would live out his vision for them to reach the world.

Try rewriting the prayer in your own words, as you pray for your own children.

For Those in Youth Ministry

If someone were to ask you today which lost teenagers you're faithfully praying for, would you have an answer?

Have you ever tried the Ignatian method of imaginative prayer? It's praying without using words. Close your eyes and picture one of your teenage friends. What do you imagine they're doing right now? Just look at them in your mind's eye. Hold your tongue. Pray using pictures instead of words. Just look at them and allow the Lord to fill you with compassion on their behalf. Now, picture Jesus walking into the room where they are. Picture his interaction with them. Listen to what he says to them. At first it might feel like a strange way to pray, but give it a shot and see how the Lord might use it to help you pray for kids.

Pray big prayers for kids. In Luke 5:20, during the healing of the paralytic, the writer records (emphasis added), "When Jesus saw *their* faith, he said, 'Friend, your sins are forgiven.'" Who will be changed by your faith?

It's easier to pray *for* kids; it's harder to actually pray *with* them. The next time you tell kids, "I'll be praying for you," why not actually lay your hands on their shoulders and pray with them right there?

Do you have people praying for you, as you enter this war on behalf of the teenagers in your life? For the last twenty years, my grandmother's Sunday school class has adopted me as their class missionary. They regularly pray for me and encourage me. Consider going before your church and asking a prayer team to form around you as you engage in the battle for lost souls.

Are you praying for those you are in ministry with? Dietrich Bonhoeffer challenges us this way:

> A Christian fellowship lives and exists by the intercession of its members for one another, or it collapses. I can no longer condemn or hate a brother for whom I pray, no matter how much trouble he causes me. His face, that hitherto may have been strange and intolerable to me, is transformed in intercession into the countenance of a brother for whom Christ died, the face of a forgiven sinner.[2]

The Word of the Lord
"Stay wide-awake in prayer" (1 Peter 4:7 MSG).

A Prayer for Believers (based on Jesus's prayer in John 17)

Father,
I pray for _____.
He or she is yours by right.
Holy Father, guard _____ as he or she pursues
this life with you.
May my friend be one in heart and mind with you and other be-
lievers.
May your joy be evident in _____.
May my friend dwell richly in your Word.
Keep _____ from joining in the world's ways.
I'm not asking that you take my friend out of the world.
But would you guard him or her from the Evil One?
May _____ not be defined by the world.
Make my friend holy—consecrated—with the truth;
Your word is consecrating truth.
Give _____ a mission in the world.
Consecrate my friend with truth.
Through _____, I pray that the world might
believe in you. Amen.

PART FOUR: THE LONG ROAD HOME

The Story of Us: We're Not There Yet

Our kids get so fired up for road trips these days. Although they periodically still ask, "Are we there yet?" they've learned to enjoy the ride. They love the snack stops, the car games, and the new DVD player in the van. But their favorite tradition is starting each trip with the windows down, the volume up, and "Shotgun Willie" Nelson serenading us with a live rendition of "On the Road Again."

Sometimes we can get so focused on the destination that we miss the joy of the journey. Diving into the lives of teenagers is exciting, yet often filled with roadblocks and discouragement. God is good and his plans are perfect. Often the journey alongside teenagers is as much about our own relationship with Jesus as it is for our teenage friends and children. In this final section, we'll dig deeper into what the Lord might be up to in us. Let's get back on the road again. We're not quite there yet.

CHAPTER 24 || SOLO

Solitude is the furnace of transformation.
—Henri Nouwen, *The Way of the Heart:*
The Spirituality of the Desert Fathers and Mothers

OUR NEXT-DOOR neighbor Jennifer often makes us pickles. They're about as close to perfect as a pickle could possibly be. Last week she brought over a jar and told me not to open it for forty-eight hours. I stared at the thing on the counter and my mouth started sweating. But I knew the key to the perfect pickle was time in the brine. In order for the cucumber to transform, it needed to soak in the solution. And then, slowly and imperceptibly, the brine-and-vinegar mixture would work its way into the cucumber, gradually changing it into a pickle.[1]

My friend Fil has taught me tons about spiritual growth. Much like the cucumber sitting in the juice, Fil parallels our relationship to the Lord to "working on a tan." Other than a slight lapse in judgment and a four-punch pass to a strip mall tanning bed—the week before our wedding—I've actually never had a tan. But I'm told if your skin isn't as Scandinavian as mine, it doesn't take much work to get one. Basically, all that's required is to put yourself in a position where the sun can do the work.

When I carefully read the Gospels, I'm struck by how the Son of God regularly positioned himself alone before his Father. When we look at the miracles of Jesus, a clear pattern develops. It happens with almost every one recorded in the Gospels, but let's revisit one particular instance. When Jesus healed the leper, he shared in the man's shame and touched the man's skin, but there's something else he did in that first chapter of Mark that frames the whole story.

In verse 35 of that first chapter, we're told, "Very early in the morning, while it was still dark, Jesus got up, left the house and went off to a solitary place, where he prayed." Three verses later, Jesus healed the leper.

As soon as the healing takes place, both Mark and Luke record the same thing about Jesus's next steps: Despite Jesus's plea that his miracles be kept secret, "the news about him spread all the more, so that crowds of people came to hear him and to be healed of their sicknesses. But Jesus often withdrew to lonely places and prayed" (Luke 5:15–16; see also Mark 1:45).

Before the miracle, and after the miracle, what did Jesus do? He soaked in the brine. He sat in the sun. He spent solo time with his Father.

And it's not only recorded in regard to the miracle of the leper; it's all over the Gospels. Before he walked on water, Jesus spent the whole night in a prayer vigil. Before he calmed the storm, he was resting in his Father's arms. Before he began casting demons out of a boy, he was fasting and praying. Before he went to the cross, he was on his knees in the garden in communion with the Father. And even before his ministry began, he spent *forty days* on a solo trip in the wilderness.

His ministry flowed out of this solitude. His life was lived in a posture of trust in the Father. In fasting, he feasted on his relationship with the Father. His compassion, his wisdom, and his miraculous power were directly related to his intimacy with the Father.

But it wasn't a one-and-done kind of thing, even for the Son of God. The Gospel writers record that Jesus often withdrew to lonely places. It was a pattern, a habit, a discipline.

If we want to pursue middle and high schoolers with the gospel of Jesus, we too must walk alongside Jesus. We must make it a priority to get alone with God. When we're in the trenches of ministry, it's often easy to lose sight of Jesus and get sucked into the vortex of the culture around us.

Sure, it seems close to impossible to have a conversation with teenagers without their phones in their hands. But it's easy to point fingers and forget to look in the mirror. Reliable studies now show that Generation Xers (ages thirty-five to forty-nine) spend even more time on social media than millennials.[2] The truth is, most of us are constantly distracted by things of lesser importance.

Our teenage friends are overcommitted, spread thin, busier than ever, and yet bored to death. But the apples don't fall too far from the tree.

If we want to reach this distracted generation, it's going to take some diligent swimming upstream. If we want to share the gospel with teenagers, we first have to believe it ourselves. We can't give them a tour of a place we've never been. How can we hear from the Lord when we ourselves are driven by distraction?

In 1 Kings 19:11–13, we see that the Lord doesn't typically scream to get our attention:

> The LORD said, "Go out and stand on the mountain in the presence of the LORD, for the LORD is about to pass by."
>
> Then a great and powerful wind tore the mountains apart and shattered the rocks before the LORD, but the LORD was not in the wind. After the wind there was an earthquake, but the LORD was not in the earthquake. After the earthquake came a fire, but the LORD was not in the fire. And after the fire came a gentle whisper. When Elijah heard it, he pulled his cloak over his face and went out and stood at the mouth of the cave.

Our willingness to give in to distractions is often prompted by our fear of missing out. We need to know what's going on in the world, what's happening with our friends, and what the next cultural craze is. We don't want to miss out on anything. Could it be that our distractions are keeping us from missing out on the most important thing—God himself?

In order to chase, we first have to cease. If we're going to run, we first must be still. To give love away, we first must believe we are his beloved.

The voice of Jesus isn't saying, "Try harder." It's saying, "Come to me." Listen to his words in the Sermon on the Mount:

> Find a quiet, secluded place so you won't be tempted to role-play before God. Just be there as simply and honestly as you can manage. The focus will shift from you to God, and you will begin to sense his grace. (Matthew 6:6 MSG)

His invitation to us is the same as it was to his disciples after they returned from their first mission trip: "'Come with me by yourselves to a quiet place and get some rest'" (Mark 6:31).

Could it be that the greatest miracle—more than healings, exorcisms, and feeding five thousand—is that we could actually encounter the living God?

For Parents

Parenting teenagers is a battle. It likely often feels as if you're losing the war and barely able to keep your head above water. When we're maxed out, typically our time alone with the Lord is one thing that's easy to forsake. We've got to spur one another on to keep soaking in the brine and the sun. It's slow and often imperceptible, but it's crucial to our being parents who can reflect God's grace to our kids. The best gift we can give our kids is to be regularly present with the Lord.

- Do your kids ever see you spending time with your Father?

- Do you often withdraw to lonely places to pray?

For Those in Youth Ministry

You can find way more kudos and fanfare when you show up at a kid's game than when you show up solo before the Lord. But you can also find way more peace and power in making intimacy with Jesus a daily habit and source of life.

One of my heroes was a guy named Jim Rayburn. He was a rebel of sorts, a youth pastor who redefined what it looked like to chase kids with the gospel. In the late 1930s, he walked across the street from his church in Gainesville, Texas, and began meeting kids who went to the high school but who wouldn't step foot in the church. Out of that ministry began the mission of Young Life. Sections of Jim's prayer journals have been kindly shared by his family:

> Enroute (on train) and evening in New Orleans. A truly remarkable day. The Lord wonderfully enabled me to spend almost the entire day in prayer. Didn't eat lunch, but continued on in prayer as He led and it was a blessed time.

> Had the best time of prayer of my whole life tonight. Did not feel like praying but knew I needed to more than anything. Just took the Lord at his Word and went to him with everything. He gave

me great peace. As I study this thing, I am convinced that times of unrest are always due to failure in prayer.

. . . a fine prayer meeting until nearly midnight.

Rose at 4:50 this a.m. and spent from then till 6:00 a.m. in prayer. Oh how I long to go on with HIM 100%, gaining strength, grace, and wisdom for whatever each day may bring—in the stillness of His presence before the day begins. Only by His enabling grace will I ever do it! In myself I am the world's biggest flop.

Was too weary to have much prayer to-night. Oh that I might never have days "too busy" to pray.

He got me up—in answer to definite prayer and I had the most down to business time of prayer that I have had in a long time. Now for the New Year—my main objective is that 1942 shall be a "prayer year"—much more than ever before.

A wonderful half-hour of prayer this morning. I have been convicted more and more about the many days that I do not really have much time ALONE for prayer—so I have asked the Lord to get me up early and let me experience Psalm 143:8: "Let the morning bring me word of your unfailing love for I have put my trust in you. Show me the way I should go, for to you I lift up my soul." He answered and gave me a real touch this a.m."

All day in prayer. No doubt the greatest day I've ever had.[3]

Over and over again, there's evidence that Jim spent many nights—all night long—on his knees before the Lord. It's evident that Young Life began as a ministry founded in prayer and solitude, and now the Lord has used it to reach millions of kids with the gospel. It seems there's a direct correlation between solitude and multitudes.

A note from Jim Rayburn's son about his dad's journal entries above (Used by permission.)*:*

When sharing those journals I felt a bit uneasy, simply because Dad had a touch of the Spirit on him that makes praying for hours on end, or all night long, an intimate, rewarding thing rather than an extremely challenging religious exercise. He was challenged to get at it, and get up and do it, but the prayer itself I believe he enjoyed at deep levels. I realized that many Christians might try to imitate that in their own strength, and crash and burn. We too frequently have a paradigm of the Christian faith that teaches people they need to do more to please God, be more, become more, clean themselves up for him. Frankly, it's a false paradigm of the faith and it's ubiquitous. I didn't want my Dad's journal entries to contribute to that.

The Word of the Lord
"I am the vine; you are the branches. If you remain in me and I in you, you will bear much fruit; apart from me you can do nothing" (John 15:5).

A Prayer of Belonging
Sit in silence and simply repeat this brief prayer over and over:

"Abba, I belong to you."

As you breathe in, say the word *Abba*—meaning daddy. As you breathe out, say, "I belong to you."

CHAPTER 25 || SCARED

We fear men so much, because we fear God so little. One fear cures
another. When man's terror scares you, turn your thoughts to the
wrath of God.

—G. K. Chesterton

AS A college student, I spent a lot of time doing outreach ministry at Northern Durham High School. Almost every Monday, Wednesday, and Friday afternoon, I'd get out of class at 1:50 p.m. and pick up my friend and teammate Ruthie McGinn. One particular day we arrived at the senior parking lot a few minutes before the bell rang. We parked the car, closed our eyes, bowed our heads, and prayed.

"Holy Spirit, go with us as we walk through the halls of the school—"
Ruff! Ruff!

Before we were able to say, "Amen," we opened our eyes and discovered that my '88 Honda Accord was surrounded by German shepherds and police cars. At the same time, the school bell rang, and students began pouring into the parking lot. By the time the majority of kids were approaching the lot, we had our hands on the roof of my car. Meanwhile the dogs were inside sniffing for drugs. A crowd quickly gathered.

After what seemed like an eternity, the cops finally granted me permission to speak. I explained we were leaders of an on-campus club and had the principal's permission to be on school grounds. The officer made a phone call to the front office, and the next thing we knew, they were gone. Ruthie and I were left standing in the middle of the high school parking lot with hundreds of eyes fixated on us, every high schooler wondering what horrible thing we had done.

Before the cops pulled out, one of the policemen let me know someone had called 911 and reported that someone, fitting my car's description and exact license plate, was reported to be selling drugs to students after school. I never found out which kid made that call, but if I ever do, I'm going to give him a standing ovation—that's one heck of a prank.

There are always going to be discouragements that try to keep us from sharing the gospel with our teenage friends and children. I can easily make a list of reasons:

- I'm not cool enough.
- I'm inadequate.
- I'm awkward.
- I don't want to offend someone.
- I'm unqualified.
- I don't have enough training.
- I don't know what to talk about.
- I'll make a fool of myself.
- I'll forget people's names.
- I'll feel so out of place.
- I'll feel like a hypocrite.
- I'm too flawed. Too weak.
- I don't want to be rejected.
- I'm afraid.

Fear is a familiar foe. It's been around since Adam and Eve started hiding from God in the garden. It's held many in its close-fisted grip—even Jesus's disciples.

In Luke 8, Jesus and his friends took an evening boat ride out on the lake. Jesus had been teaching, healing, and performing miracles all day long. With the rocking of the boat in the water, the gentle breeze in the air, and the sunset on the horizon, of course he fell asleep. He was fully human, after all. But soon after God started snoring, the weather conditions changed. That's how it always seemed to happen on the Sea of Galilee.

> A squall came down on the lake, so that the boat was being swamped, and they were in great danger.
>
> The disciples went and woke Jesus, saying, "Master, Master, we're going to drown!"
>
> He got up and rebuked the wind and the raging waters; the storm subsided, and all was calm. "Where is your faith?" he asked his disciples.

In fear and amazement they asked one another, "Who is this? He commands even the winds and the water, and they obey him." (Luke 8:23–25)

I wonder how they woke him up. Do you shake the Son of God? Or do you just whisper in his ear? And when he finally woke, did he blink a few times and take a moment to rub the sleep from his eyes? Was he in a hurry? Did God stretch and yawn?

In the middle of that mammoth lake, their boat was being attacked with the fury of pounding rain and thunder like cannonballs. The high winds shook the sails. Water began to fill the boat. Everyone panicked.

Then, Jesus stood up. In the middle of a rocking ship. And raised his hands and voice. And with simply a word, creation bowed to its Master.

But Jesus didn't just calm the wind and waves; he also silenced the disciples' screams. As the dark clouds parted and the stars began to shine through, the same calmness filled these twelve friends. Sitting there soaking wet, drenched by the storm, their grip began to loosen from the bars of the boat. With his presence, Jesus had replaced their fear of the world with a fear of the man who'd been sleeping in the stern.

"In fear and amazement they asked one another, 'Who is this?'" The storm scared them, but the calm terrified them.[1]

Fear is the greatest enemy of evangelism. But the remedy for the fear of the world is a holy fear of the Almighty God.

There's a consistent pattern in Scripture of what happens in a life that God wants to use. It's a pattern of a call followed by a fear. God calls an ordinary person to engage in an act of extraordinary trust, and that person naturally experiences fear. It seems God has a habit of asking people to do things that are scary to them.[2] Why would a loving God do that?

I recently took some high school guys cliff jumping off waterfalls in the North Carolina mountains. One of the older guys surprised me and refused to jump. I debated just letting it go, but I knew it was safe and he'd regret not giving it a shot, so I pushed him. I pushed him hard. Not with my hands, but with my words. And he wasn't happy with me, but he did it. And finally, after he came up out of the water, the tenseness in his face had melted to laughter.

Usually, when we're afraid of something God is calling us to do, we can expect that same pattern to occur. It starts with us refusing to jump. And then, eventually giving in. And then, we finally get to experience the joy of obedience.

God is calling all of us to be a part of something much larger than ourselves. He's inviting us into his God-sized plans. He knows we're creatures of comfort. And he's aware that sharing the gospel with teenagers is out of that comfort zone. But he also knows that comfort hinders growth. And his deepest desire for us is that we would grow and be transformed into his likeness.

My childhood pastor, Dr. Gary Chapman, wrote a book called *The Five Love Languages*.[3] It's one of the most helpful relationship tools I've ever seen. The book helps explain how to best care for those you love by speaking their *love language*. Some people appreciate words of affirmation. My wife feels most loved by quality time. I love when others do acts of service for me. Others value physical touch or receiving gifts. I'm convinced that God has a love language too. It's faith. God feels the most loved by us when we demonstrate absolute trust in him. God moves toward us with love, but we move toward him with faith.

There are hundreds of verses in the Scriptures that point to this reality, but one particularly makes me pause. In all of the Gospels, there is only one place where Jesus is recorded as being amazed. And the person who amazed Jesus happened to be a Roman soldier:

> He was not far from the house when the centurion sent friends to say to him: "Lord, don't trouble yourself, for I do not deserve to have you come under my roof. That is why I did not even consider myself worthy to come to you. But say the word, and my servant will be healed. For I myself am a man under authority, with soldiers under me. I tell this one, 'Go,' and he goes; and that one, 'Come,' and he comes. I say to my servant, 'Do this,' and he does it."
>
> When Jesus heard this, he was amazed at him, and turning to the crowd following him, he said, "I tell you, I have not found such great faith even in Israel." (Luke 7:6–9)

When we display faith in the midst of our fear, it makes Jesus marvel.

But it also makes the teenagers in our lives pause in wonder. Our faith demonstrates to teenagers how we can actually love God. It puts our money where our mouths are.

For Parents

- Look back over the parts of the book you've underlined. What have you felt *prompted* by the Lord to do, yet have not found the courage to *actually* do?

- What are you currently doing that requires faith?

- Are your kids watching you take any risks? Step out of your comfort zone.

- How does the way you spend your time and money reflect a life abandoned in absolute trust of God?

- Do you ever talk to your kids about your own fears? Do you keep it real with them? How do you teach them to handle being afraid?

For Those in Youth Ministry

What are your biggest fears when it comes to youth ministry? Have you talked about them with anyone on your ministry teams? Acknowledging those fears is the first step to moving past them.

How do we overcome these fears?

- We remember that the Lord has called us and is with us.
- We remember that, despite our faults, God has still chosen us as his ambassadors (2 Corinthians 4:7).
- We remember that kids are dying for adult friends and looking for older folks they can talk to and trust.

The Word of the Lord

"For the Spirit God gave us does not make us timid, but gives us power, love and self-discipline" (2 Timothy 1:7).

A Prayer for Faith

Lord,
Give us a faith that makes you marvel.
We know you are the author and perfecter of our faith, and that even the ability to trust you is a gift from you.
We know that you are the only One we have to fear, but that your plans for us are good.
Lord, pursuing teenagers is hard. It's often heartbreaking, disappointing, demanding, exhausting, and humbling. But it's also full of hope, excitement, adventure, and deep joy.
In our moments of fear, give us faith in the One who is always faithful.
In our moments of impatience, give us faith in the One who's timing is perfect.
In our moments of discouragement, give us faith in the One who endured the cross on the way to an empty tomb.
Oh Lord, give us faith. Amen.

CHAPTER 26 || STRINGS

The mark of a heart that has been touched by the Grace of God
will inevitably be led to deeds of compassion to the neediest, most
broken, the most ungrateful, and the kind of person who is furthest
away from you demographically, socially, racially, and every other way.
—Tim Keller

ONE AFTERNOON, the Middle Eastern sun was beating down on Jesus and his
disciples as they climbed the mountain to Jerusalem. Suddenly, they saw in
the distance a group of ten men, all of whom had leprosy.

When the men realized it was the healer everyone was talking about,
they starting screaming, "Jesus, Master, have pity on us!"

Unlike when he had healed the other leper in Mark 1, Jesus didn't touch
these men. He simply healed them with his words.

He instructed them: "Go, show yourselves to the priests."

A leper was considered unclean and not welcome inside the city, much
less in the temple courts. Never before had these men been able to even approach a priest, but now, their sores had all vanished before their eyes. They
ran with confidence, because now they had the freedom to go before the priest
and be declared clean. No longer would they be outcasts. No longer would
they be dirty. Now, they could be held by loved ones, and accepted by all.

Now as one of the lepers—a Samaritan—was running with the others,
he realized how his life had been forever changed. The Scriptures say that
"when he saw he was healed, [he] came back, praising God in a loud voice.
He threw himself at Jesus's feet and thanked him" (Luke 17:15).

Then Jesus asked him a question. "'Were not all ten cleansed? Where are
the other nine? Has no one else returned to give praise to God except this
foreigner?'" (Luke 17:11–18).

And then, Jesus used his magic to reverse the healing on the other nine
and struck them down with even more sores than they had before. Or . . .

none of that happened—no magic spells, no reversal of healing, no intensified symptoms, no comeuppance at all.

Jesus loved with no strings attached. Of course, he desired the praise he was rightfully due, but he gave healing that was undeserved, even with the knowledge that there would be no gratitude displayed.

We often play games in our families and with our friends. We offer compliments that are essentially requests for admiration returned. We give gifts that are actually more about us receiving admiration than they are about the receiver being loved. We hand out favors, secretly expecting to cash in on what we're owed sometime down the road.

Jesus handed out miracles. Jesus handed out grace. Jesus handed out love. With no strings attached.

In 2010, Natalie and I fell in love with the Braverman family on our all-time favorite TV show, *Parenthood*. One episode of the show focused on two of the main characters, Joel and Julia, and their attempt to adopt a ten-year-old Hispanic boy named Victor. One day, about a week before his adoption was finalized, Victor was running through the house playing football and accidentally smashed an expensive vase. Julia, his mom-to-be, hears the crash and races into the room.

"I'm sorry. I'll pay for it," Victor says.

Julia responds, "It's OK, you don't have to pay for it. Let's just go back to the no-football-in-the-house rule."

Victor then asks, "So you're not going to change your mind about adopting me?"

Julia replies, "No. I'm never going to change my mind."

Vic simply said, "OK." The fear melted off his face. And his smile stretched across the screen.

There is something so freeing about being loved with no strings attached. But let's be honest—well, at least let *me* be honest. That's not been my MO. The love I've dished out has often looked way more like a marionette show than an unconditional gift.

Confession time: I had poured my heart out at these high schools and longed to be recognized for the many hours I'd so *selflessly* (insert sarcastic emoji) volunteered. For the longest time in youth ministry, I had this super-unhealthy fantasy: I secretly wanted the yearbook to be dedicated to me. I've never actually admitted that out loud to anyone, but for almost a decade, on the day the yearbook came out, I would first flip to the dedication page and see if my picture was there. When that goal was never met, I started keeping tallies of how many times my picture would at least appear elsewhere in the book. As a twenty-something in youth ministry, it seemed like a trophy—proof that I was actually making an impact.

Then, there was the rich-kid season. I was raising support, and it was fairly easy to quickly tell which kids at the high school had money. When choosing to spend time with rich Rick or single-mom Sam, the strategic choice was obvious. And it worked—many of those wealthier kids' parents did support me, and I'm grateful. But I'm also ashamed.

But it wasn't just money that attracted me to pursue certain kids; it was also potential fame. I made friends with kids who had promise of being somebody—an athlete, an actor, a musician. I wanted my name in their liner notes someday.

And then I fell into a trap I never even saw coming: I'll help really *poor* kids. I'll reach out to the outcasts and the nobodies. Man, that sure will make me look good.

As a seminary student, I continued to do youth ministry and kept on sinking in my need to be admired. At the time, I was regularly meeting with a couple mentors, Bob and Pete. Much to my surprise, they weren't too impressed with me. One day, Bob called me on the carpet and told me I needed to see a counselor. He was so convinced that he offered to pay for it.

I walked into the counselor's office planning to make another friend. But before our hour had expired, I'd been exposed. She opened the DSM-5, the *Diagnostic and Statistical Manual of Mental Disorders*, and began reading characteristics of a person with Narcissistic Personality Disorder.[1]

- An exaggerated sense of self-importance
- Expecting to be recognized as superior, even without achievements that warrant it
- Exaggerating achievements and talents
- Being preoccupied with fantasies about success, power, brilliance, beauty, or the perfect mate
- Believing you are superior and can only be understood by, or associate with, equally special people
- Requiring constant admiration
- Having a sense of entitlement
- Expecting special favors and unquestioning compliance with your expectations

- Taking advantage of others to get what you want
- Having an inability or unwillingness to recognize the needs and feelings of others
- Being envious of others, and believing others envy you
- Behaving in an arrogant or haughty manner

It was as if she held up a mirror and I watched it painfully crack. Thankfully, by God's grace, I do not have NPD, but confronting those narcissistic traits in my own life was an unpleasant wake-up call.

On the outside, I looked like I was loving people so well. But on the inside, I was rotting away in self-obsession.

Even ministry can become an idol. Even parenting can become way more about us than about our kids. We must remind ourselves that kids aren't trophies to be won over or hoisted on our mantles. Sharing the gospel is not a competition. It's way more like jumping in a river than climbing up a ladder.

For Parents

- Have you personally felt manipulated by love? Do you feel as if your own parents loved you with strings attached?

- When have you shown your kids conditional love? When have you treated them differently based on their performance? Do you need to apologize to them?

For Those in Youth Ministry

- Do you ever choose who you pursue based on what they can do for you?

- Do you recognize any of the self-centered tendencies in the DSM listing above? Confess them to the Lord. Pray the prayer of humility below, and personalize it to make it your own.

The Word of the Lord

"Am I now trying to win the approval of human beings, or of God? Or am I trying to please people? If I were still trying to please people, I would not be a servant of Christ" (Galatians 1:10).

A Prayer for Humility in Ministry

Jesus,
I need a humble heart, but I barely know how to ask.
Lord, break me of my self-centeredness.
May I become so convinced that you love me, with no strings attached, that, in turn, I have the grace to love others the same way.
May I live not for the applause of men but for the applause of you.
Loving others and expecting nothing in return.
May I hear your voice and your approval louder than the sirens of the world. Exchange my need for praise with a heart that longs to praise you.
This is my prayer as I bow before you now. Amen.

CHAPTER 27 || STRATEGY

Jesus was deeply concerned for the continuation of his redemptive work after the close of his earthly existence, and his chosen method was simply a formation of a small band of committed friends.

—Elton Trueblood

BILLY GRAHAM was once asked what his strategy would be if he were the pastor of a large church. He responded that he would follow the pattern that Christ set and spend most of his time with twelve guys and give them everything he had.[1]

Mother Teresa was once asked the question, "How did you rescue fifty thousand people off the streets of Calcutta?"

She responded this way: "I started with one."[2]

Before Jesus's ascension into heaven, his disciples no doubt wondered, "What's the last thing you want us to know and do before you ascend to heaven?" His response to that concern went like this: "Go and make disciples of all nations, baptizing them in the name of the Father and of the Son and of the Holy Spirit, and teaching them to obey everything I have commanded you" (Matthew 28:19–20).

That's the strategy of Jesus. Making disciples. Quaker theologian Elton Trueblood puts it this way:

> There is no person in history who has impacted all of humankind more than Jesus of Nazareth.
>
> Jesus was deeply concerned for the continuation of his redemptive work after the close of his earthly existence, and his chosen method was simply a formation of a small band of committed friends.
>
> He did not form an army, establish a headquarters, or even write a book. What he did was collect a few very common men and women, inspire them with the sense of the spirit and vision, and build their lives into an intensive fellowship of affection, worship, and work.

[In the Sermon on the Mount], Jesus indicates that there is absolutely no substitute for the tiny, loving, caring, reconciling society. If this fails, he suggests, all is a failure; there is no other way. He told the little bedraggled fellowship that they were actually the salt of the earth and that if this salt should fail there would be no adequate preservative at all. He was staking it all on one throw.

What we need is not intellectual theorizing or even preaching, but a demonstration. One of the most powerful ways of turning people's loyalty to Christ is by loving others with the great love of God. We cannot revive faith by argument, but we might catch the imagination of puzzled men and women by an exhibition of a fellowship so intensely alive that every thoughtful person would be forced to respect it. If there should emerge in our day such a fellowship, wholly without artificiality and free from the dead hand of the past, it would be an exciting event of momentous importance. A society of genuine loving souls, set free from the self-seeking struggle for personal prestige and from all unreality, would be something unutterably priceless and powerful. A wise person would travel any distance to join it.[3]

If we want to spread the gospel the *Jesus way*, then that's our road map. We go both deeper and wider. We go deep by actually making disciples. We go wider by reaching all nations. Every kind of kid. Everywhere.

And we add by multiplication, instead of addition. We make disciples who make disciples.

Most of Jesus's ministry was spent with just twelve guys. And when we read stories about Jesus, there is more recorded about his time with the disciples than even the multitudes of people he ministered to. And even of those twelve, he just chose three—Peter, James, and John—and went deep. He walked with them, ate with them, rebuked them, laughed with them, prayed with them, and told them about his Father.

That's the same invitation he has given us.

For Parents

The most important prayer in Judaism is called the *Shema*. It is known by the Hebrew word meaning *hear*, which begins this familiar passage in Deuteronomy 6:4–9:

Hear, O Israel: The LORD our God, the LORD is one. Love the LORD your God with all your heart and with all your soul and with all your strength. These commandments that I give you today are to be on your hearts. Impress them on your children. Talk about them when you sit at home and when you walk along the road, when you lie down and when you get up. Tie them as symbols on your hands and bind them on your foreheads. Write them on the doorframes of your houses and on your gates.

The Shema prayer is spoken daily in Jewish tradition and was so important that Jesus used these very words as the beginning of his answer to the question: What is the greatest commandment? (Mark 12:29–30).

As a parent, it's pretty clear God has called our children to be included in our band of disciples. And the greatest commandment he has given us involves us not only loving God, but also writing his love and his law on the hearts of our kids. Eugene Peterson translates the above passage this way: "Write these commandments that I've given you today on your hearts. Get them inside of you and then get them inside your children" (Deuteronomy 6:6–7 MSG).

One of our children recently struggled with some pretty intense nighttime anxiety. Last week, when I was reading to her before bed, I noticed some new graffiti on the underside of the top bunk. Without me knowing, Natalie had written Scripture on the wood for her to read as she tried to fall asleep. Truth about God, his presence, and his dominion over fear. She had taken the *Shema* literally and written the Word on the (bed)frames of our house.

This week, I met with some parents who were overwhelmed by the pace of their high schooler's life. It seems there is no break in the chaos, no rest from the treadmill, and no rhythm in their family's schedule. I get it. Life is full. Parenting is hard.

As we continued to chat, I felt prompted to ask them about the fourth commandment. I first confessed my own failure to remember the Sabbath day and keep it holy.

But then I asked, "Have you as parents clearly established a pattern of Sabbath rest in your home? Have you modeled that for your kids?" I reminded them that it wasn't too late to start.

The key to discipling children is for us as parents to actually live the lives we're inviting them into.

For Those in Youth Ministry

- What's your current strategy in youth ministry? How does it line up with the strategy of Jesus? What needs to be tweaked?

- Who are your multitudes?

- Who are your crowds?

- Who are your twelve?

- Who are your Peter, James, and John?

- Who is training *you*?

If you can't answer the questions above, meet with a more experienced mentor in ministry and ask him or her to help you process how the Lord might be calling you to intentionally walk alongside teenagers in a formative process of discipleship.

The Word of the Lord

"You then, my son, be strong in the grace that is in Christ Jesus. And the things you have heard me say in the presence of many witnesses entrust to reliable people who will also be qualified to teach others" (2 Timothy 2:1–2).

A Prayer for the Nations

> Almighty God,
> The harvest is plentiful, but the workers are few. I ask you, Lord, to send workers into the field.
> Give me a compassionate heart for the lost. Give me a desire for the salvation of the nations.
> Remove my spirit of fear and replace it with power and love and discipline. Remove my anxiety and replace it with peace.
> Lord Jesus Christ, you stretched out your arms of love on the hard wood of the cross, that everyone might come within the reach of your saving embrace. Clothe us in your Spirit that we, reaching forth our hands in love, may bring those who do not know you to the knowledge and love of you—for the honor of your name. Amen.

CHAPTER 28 || SQUAD

The person who loves their dream of community will destroy community, but the person who loves those around them will create community.
—Dietrich Bonhoeffer, *Life Together: The Classic Exploration of Christian Community*

I SPOKE on the phone with my friend Ted Woodard yesterday. I haven't seen him in probably a decade. We still talk a couple times a year but now live across the country from each other.

Last night I told Natalie, "Even though I never see him, and even after all these years, I just love that guy." I then asked her, "Why do you think my heart feels so tied to his?" After some discussion, it became apparent what the main factors were. Ted and I were soldiers together in a really difficult year of ministry. We battled together, fought together, cried together, and still share that same passion for lost teenagers.

Our goal as we make disciples is to bring them face-to-face with Jesus, but also to invite them into a missional community—a community of people, living together with the same purpose.

There's nothing more bonding than being on mission together. You've probably felt that. Think back over the mission trips you've been on. The ministry teams. People you've labored with in missional community.

But community can easily get too caught up in itself; that's why it has to be missional. You've seen it happen with churches that gradually become more like members-only country clubs. They didn't start that way; they didn't intend to grow that way, but that's the slope we live on, so that's the way the ball is naturally going to roll if we're not paying attention.

One of my former seminary professors models this with his life. He's one of the best-known biblical scholars on the planet, yet he doesn't live in his office or a library. He's a man who gets his hands dirty and feeds the homeless. He eats dinner with those who look way different from him. He gives his money away to the poor. If anyone has a right to speak on this topic, it's Craig Blomberg. He writes, "Christian fellowship should be a periodic retreat from and revitalization of our regular involvement with the immoral and unbelieving in our world and not vice versa."[1]

Community is vital, but it must be community *on mission*. Being on mission together is different than hanging out in a safe bubble. Here are three questions to help you hold the line:

1. Are we falling more in love with God? Hungering more for God?
2. Are we falling more in love with one another?
3. Are we falling more in love with the lost?

And just as Jesus is the example in our incarnational approach to ministry, he is our example in terms of a team ministry as well. Jesus gathered people around him for a clear purpose. "He appointed twelve that they might be with him and that he might send them out to preach" (Mark 3:14).

He modeled for us the pattern of doing ministry together. He didn't need the disciples, but it was Jesus's way. Just as the Trinity functions in perfect love, Jesus modeled doing ministry in community.

He also sent out the disciples in pairs. Paul writes in 1 Corinthians 12 and Ephesians 4 about the importance of the different parts that make up the body. As we do ministry together, it's vital that we all have different gifts and abilities. Often, the best teams are made up of people who wouldn't normally be friends apart from Christ.

Affinity-driven friendships easily become inward focused. Friendships that happen as a result of the gospel more naturally remain on mission. When we love one another like this, it's a megaphone for the gospel. Jesus told his disciples, "A new command I give you: Love one another. As I have loved you, so you must love one another. By this everyone will know that you are my disciples, if you love one another" (John 13:34–35).

When we actually see ministry teams functioning like this, it's one of the most beautiful gospel pictures we'll ever witness. And when you see it, you'll long to be a part of it.

For Parents

When it comes to discipling children, God gave the gift of marriage to form the front-line squad. Yet, we live in a culture where marriage is under critical attack. The enemy loves to bring down families by dividing husband and wife. If you are married, prioritize your spouse over your children. It's one of the greatest gifts you can give them. When kids see a united front between their parents, it makes them feel safe and loved. Remember the words of Jesus: "By this [your kids] will know that you are my disciples, if you love one another."

Consider taking the chapters that have stood out to you in this book and inviting your spouse to read them so you can discuss and make a game-plan together.

For those of you who are single parents, you are not alone. When Jesus came into the world, he redefined family. Listen to what happened in Matthew 12:46–50:

> While Jesus was still talking to the crowd, his mother and brothers stood outside, wanting to speak to him. Someone told him, "Your mother and brothers are standing outside, wanting to speak to you."
>
> He replied to him, "Who is my mother, and who are my brothers?" Pointing to his disciples, he said, "Here are my mother and my brothers. For whoever does the will of my Father in heaven is my brother and sister and mother."

Jesus created the church to be the family of God. If you're a single parent, be bold in seeking out other adults in your local church to partner with you in discipling your children. Parenting is not a solo sport. In faith, ask the Lord to provide and, in faith, make your needs known to the church.

One of our greatest blessings as parents has been the gift of our weekly small group. Every other week, for the past seven years, we've gathered with the same four other families. We've spent close to two hundred evenings together laughing, feasting, praying, crying, fighting, and learning how to follow Jesus together. We've walked through miscarriages and the death of parents. We've taken parenting classes, watched parenting videos, and read parenting books together. But honestly, the most helpful thing we've done is simply parent our kids alongside one another, rejoicing together in small victories and learning from one another's mistakes. We weren't designed to do this alone. We all need a squad.

For Those in Youth Ministry
If you are reading this section of the book, odds are you fall into one of these three categories:

1. You do youth ministry alone and are desperately longing for a squad.
2. You do youth ministry on a team and yet still feel alone.
3. You do youth ministry on a team and feel supported, connected, and loved.

If you're not yet at number three, do not dismay. The Lord wants you to be on a team. He has good plans for you. He is up to something in and through you.

In addition to praying specifically for a team, here are a few other steps you could take:

- Develop a support team of people who love and care about you. Maybe they will not actually get in the trenches with you. Maybe they live in a different state. But they can still pray and support you from afar. Send them regular updates with specific ways they can pray for you and for kids in your ministry.
- Talk to your pastor, the director of your parachurch ministry, or other Christian leaders in your community. Let them know you're feeling alone. Ask them to help you brainstorm potential teammates.
- Connect with others doing youth ministry in your home. Even if it's a different church or parachurch ministry, odds are there are others experiencing the same emotions you are.

If you are on a number-three team, thank God for that amazing gift. After that, use some of the questions below to help take your team deeper into missional community:

- When have you watched a teammate demonstrate Jesus's love to one of his or her middle- or high-school friends?
- If our team could improve on one aspect of ministry, what would it be?
- What's one thing you would like to improve in your personal ministry next year?
- What is one thing we can be accountable for to help you grow personally and in your ministry? How can we as a team support you?
- What sacrifices are you making to do youth ministry? Are those wise sacrifices to make?
- Who are potential leaders you can be praying for who might join your team?
- How do we feel about our team dynamics?
  - Do we love one another well?
  - Pray for one another consistently?

     o   Serve and help one another?
     o   How can we grow in these areas?
- If a ministry team leader is leading this time:
  - What is something I as a team leader am doing well?
  - What is something I as a team leader can improve?

The Word of the Lord

"A new command I give you: Love one another. As I have loved you, so you must love one another. By this everyone will know that you are my disciples, if you love one another" (John 13:34–35).

A Prayer for Unity

We are gathered here because we believe that we are called together into a work we cannot yet know the fullness of.

And so we offer to you, O God, these things: Our dreams, our plans, our vision.

Shape them as you will. Our moments and our gifts. May they now be invested toward bright, eternal ends.

Richly bless the work before us, Father, giving grace lest we grow enamored by our own accomplishment or entrenched in old habit.

Instead, let us be ever listening for your voice, ever open to the quiet beckoning of your Spirit in this endeavor.

You alone, O God, by your gracious and life-giving Spirit, have power to knit our imperfect hearts, our weaknesses, our strengths, our stories, and our gifts, one to the other.

Unite your people and multiply our meager offerings, O Lord, that all might resound to your glory.

May our love and our labors now echo your love and your labors, O Lord.

Let all that we do here, in these our brief lives, in this our brief moment to love, in this, the work you have ordained for this community, flower in winsome and beautiful foretaste of still greater glories yet to come.

O Spirit of God, now shape our hearts.

O Spirit of God, now guide our hands.

O Spirit of God, now build your kingdom among us. Amen.[2]

CHAPTER 29 || SLOW

"I will tell you a further mystery," he said. "It may take longer."
—Wendell Berry, *Jayber Crow*

JAYBER CROW, a fictional character created by Wendell Berry, was born in Goforth, Kentucky, orphaned at age ten, began his search as a pre-ministerial student at Pigeonville College. There, freedom met with new burdens, and a young man needed more than a mirror to find himself. But the beginning of that finding was a short conversation with Old Grit, his profound professor of New Testament Greek:

> "You have been given questions to which you cannot be given answers. You will have to live them out—perhaps a little at a time."
> "And how long is that going to take?"
> "I don't know. As long as you live, perhaps."
> "That could be a long time."
> "I will tell you a further mystery," he said. "It may take longer."[1]

The Lord rarely works on our timetable. It takes ten years for grapes to become mature wine. Joseph was locked up for at least thirteen years before he came into power. The Israelites wandered for forty years in the desert before entering the promised land. Jesus spent thirty years in preparation for three years of ministry.

It seems the Lord's strategy isn't just multiplication and community. It seems his strategy is patience.

Jesus was never in a hurry.

One difficult thing about both parenting and ministry is this desire to see dramatic life change happen overnight. While those instances do sometimes occur, I'm learning that far more often, our journey toward Christ happens in small, often imperceptible steps. Perhaps, this is how God keeps us humble.

A year ago, I was in the most discouraged place I'd ever been in ministry. I felt as if I'd been doing it for so long and seen so little fruit.

"Has anything I've done actually mattered?" I'd recently found out that a kid I had invested in had taken his own life at age thirty-three. I was beating myself up for not reaching out to him more recently, and honestly, I just wanted to quit.

But one Wednesday in August, I was driving to a meeting in Charlotte and got ambushed by God.

I got a call from a young man named Greg that I hadn't spoken to in a decade. He Facebook messaged me the previous week and asked for my number. Fifteen years ago, I did youth ministry in his hometown. Sometimes, Greg would show up with his friends, but we were never super close. When Natalie and I moved to Colorado for seminary, we lost touch.

I drove down I-85 and the phone rang. And Greg started telling me about his last decade—how he ran from God and got a girl pregnant, which led to an abortion. He became an alcoholic, couldn't get into college, got in a major fight with his dad, and ended up moving to Texas to work on an oil rig. A few years later Greg was finally able to go to college, and through a college ministry, he met Jesus. Then, his whole world changed.

Now he was teaching high school, coaching football, and thinking about going into youth ministry. He told me he wanted to call and thank me for chasing him back in the day. He said when he was just a middle-school kid, I was the first person who ever showed him a glimpse of Jesus.

I hung up the phone, crying, and just worshiped the Lord.

Then, I got to the meeting in Charlotte and had a guy come up to me and ask if we could talk. He told me he was leading a ministry at a brand-new high school in a neighboring city and that the principal of the school completely opened the doors for them to do ministry there. He even invited them to have meetings that were all about Jesus, right there in a classroom of a public high school. He told me the reason the principal was so open to them being there was because he'd been pursued by me when he was in high school years ago.

I just started shaking. The kindness of the Lord was overwhelming.

I hadn't talked to that kid since he graduated from high school. I had no clue he was even following the Lord, much less that he was the principal of a school.

Now these stories are not the norm, but they were a gift. They were a reminder to wait on the Lord because his timing is always perfect. It's crazy to think we only really know the name *Lazarus* because Jesus showed up "too late."

The takeaways from these pages can't all be done at once. Don't "should" on yourself. You don't have to prove yourself. Rest in the grace of God. Listen to the holder of your heart. Take small, deliberate, and consistent steps toward him and the teenagers in your life. Play the long game.

Natalie and I were recently sitting in our den with our friends Bill and Joann Goans, seeking God's wisdom for these pages. They've been doing ministry in the same neighborhood, high school, and city for close to forty years.

In Bill's gentle southern drawl, these are the last words he said to me before we prayed and they headed home: "I can't say enough about the impact of following Christ in the same place over many years. It's way more important than your abilities. Over the long haul, faithfulness is way more important than giftedness. I'm not saying that gifts don't mean anything, but they're a bit overrated."

If you've made it this far in the book, it's obvious you want to be in this for the long haul. That you want to be so convinced of the Father's love for you that you can keep running after kids with all you've got until the day you meet Jesus face-to-face.

The Lord is faithful, even when we're not. After all, he's the God who's been walking alongside us all along. And he's patiently waiting for those teenagers we so dearly love. Like the father of the prodigal son, he sits on the porch, eyes on the horizon. And when the moment comes, he'll leap over that railing and then we'll get to watch God run.

A Prayer for Teenagers

Good Lord,
Give us the teenagers that we may lead them to Thee.
Our hearts ache for the millions of young people who remain untouched by the gospel and for the tragically large proportion of those who have dropped by the wayside and find themselves without spiritual guidance.
Help us to give them a chance, oh Father, a chance to become aware of thy Son's beauty and healing power in the might of the Holy Spirit.
Oh, Lord Jesus, give us the teenagers, each one at least long enough for a meaningful confrontation with Thee.
We are at best unprofitable servants, but thy grace is sufficient.
Oh, thou Holy Spirit, give us the teenagers.
For we love them and know them to be awfully lonely.
Dear Lord, give us the teenagers.[2]

APPENDIX: PRACTICAL TOOLS FOR WORKING WITH TEENAGERS

Helpful Questions and Icebreakers

Light

- If you really knew me, you would know . . .
- What are the highs and lows of your week so far?
- What are some of your pet peeves?
- Tell me a few songs you are loving right now.
- What three websites do you spend the most time on?
- What movie or TV character do you most identify with and why?
- Show me five of the last twenty pictures in your camera, and explain each picture.
- What's one of the best gifts you've ever received?
- Where do you see yourself in ten years?
- What's the best or worst vacation you've ever been on?
- With which famous person would you most like to share a meal? What would you ask him or her?
- If you got a tattoo, what would it be and where?
- What is your earliest memory?
- Who was your childhood hero and why?
- Would you rather give a compliment or receive a compliment?

Deep

- How do you think God feels about you?
- How would you describe your relationship with Christ right now?
- In what area of your life do you feel most satisfied or empty right now? Why?

- If you had to live this past week over again, would you change anything? If so, what?
- What is one way your parents have sacrificed for you?
- Finish the sentence: If you lived in my house for a week you might be surprised by . . .
- Finish the sentence: I wish God would . . .
- What are three to five words your parents would use to describe you? Your friends would use? You would use?
- If you could have any question answered, what would it be?
- What has been your biggest disappointment?
- Who knows you best?
- Do you see yourself as a leader or a follower? Why?
- When have you made your mom or dad proud?
- What have you been praying for this week?
- I heard you say _____. Tell me more about that.
- What do you think God has been trying to teach you lately?
- Tell me about an adult (teacher, coach, et cetera) who has influenced your life, and in what ways.
- What's been one of the scariest moments in your life?
- Tell me the names of your family members, and describe your relationship with them.
- If you knew you wouldn't fail, what's one thing you would like to do in life?
- At your funeral, what do you want people to say about you?
- What is one thing you wish you could change about yourself?
- In what area of your life do you feel the most stressed out?
- Finish the sentence: One thing that makes me angry is . . .
- What's the hardest part of being a teenager?

Deeper
- My best day ever was . . .
- My worst days ever was . . .
- What is one regret you have that no one in this room knows about?
- What one thing has helped you grow most in your relationship with Christ?
- Where do you feel the greatest spiritual challenge?
- If you could erase one memory from your past, what would it be?
- When is the last time you cried, and why?
- When is the last time you apologized to someone, and why?
- When is a time you've felt closest to God?

- When is a time you've felt farthest away from God?
- When is a time you really needed God?
- What is an important conversation that has shaped your life?
- What makes it hard for you to follow Jesus?
- What motivates you to follow Jesus?
- What is the biggest mental battle you face?

Tips on Doing Surprise Wake-Up Videos (Chapter 12)

Pick the Right Kids to Wake Up

- Don't necessarily pick the kids who are always on stage at youth group or at Young Life club. Give some other kids a chance to shine.
- Select siblings and get twice the bang for your buck. This only works if they share a room (or have rooms far apart enough that one sibling won't be tipped off when the other is surprised). The wake-up is loud and usually will wake up the other sibling while you are waking the first one. If this is probable, get one sibling in on it ahead of time and have him or her help you wake up the brother or sister.
- You only have a short window of time before school, so pick kids who live near one another. If you're going to wake up one kid at five thirty in the morning and another who lives fifteen minutes away, you might be too late. Attempt to find multiple kids in the same neighborhood to limit your early mornings.

Contact Parents

- Call them ahead of time, when their kids are at school, or email them to avoid the awkward, "Why did my leader just call you?" question to the parents. Most parents will love this, and it's a great way to get them involved. It's fun and shows parents how committed we are to their kids.
- Confirm time of your arrival with parents so they are waiting and not surprised themselves.
- Make sure that if they have a dog, it won't bark when you arrive and wake the kids.

Use Skit Characters

- Search YouTube for *Good Morning Young Life* for tons of funny ideas. Consider using news broadcasters who do the morning show, or find a giant hot dog, Big Bird, banana suit, or some other funny costume.

Same Gender

- Make sure you have at least one leader of the same gender as the high schooler or middle schooler you are waking up. It's not appropriate for two female leaders to go wake up a high school guy and vice versa.

Film in the Driveway

- It's funny to arrive early and do your run-on repeater lines in the driveway of the kid's house. If it is still dark outside, make sure you have some sort of light to shine on the character, so he or she will be visible.

Funny Commentary

- When you enter the house, get some video footage of funny childhood pictures on the walls of the kids you are waking up. Plan some funny commentary about the pictures. If you're nervous about the kid hearing you, just do this after the wake-up.

Use Funny Props to Wake Kids Up

- Leaf blower (electric—gas-powered blowers will make the house reek of gas). This is especially funny on kids with long hair that will blow everywhere and also if you get a close-up shot of it blowing in the kid's mouth.
- Air horn.
- Pot and metal spoon.
- Portable loud Bluetooth speaker using a song that starts loud and fun, possibly your run-on character's theme song. I've also used the beginning of "Circle of Life" from *The Lion King*. It starts loud and abruptly! You could use the theme song from the old school show "Saved by the Bell" and make it the traditional "Good Morning Wake-Up" song.
- Bullhorn. Awesome to use, not as easy to find. Check with your local megachurch that has a gym. Chances are they will own one and let you borrow it.

Light Switch

- Ask the parents where the light switch is in their kid's room. Sadly, I've filmed videos where I couldn't find the light switch and it was too dark to catch the kid's expression. It's tough if the kid uses an overhead light that is controlled by a pull string on the ceiling fan or a bright lamp in a corner. Plan ahead. Lighting is essential!

Proper PJs

- Ask the parents what their child typically sleeps in. I have accidentally woken up kids wearing only underwear. This can be awkward, but avoidable if you just make sure the covers stay on them while you are in the room with them. I'd also recommend leaving the room immediately after you get the video of them waking up, to give them some time to get ready.

Morning Calisthenics

- After victims have had a minute to gather themselves from the surprise, use this time to do some funny morning exercises with them. Potentially use the wake-up videos as a way to sell camp. Tell them that "camp is physically demanding; you're going to be doing high-risk and high-energy activities that require you to be in tip-top physical condition!" Name some of the rides at camp. Video the skit characters leading the student in morning push-ups, jumping jacks, and so on. If the student has a trampoline or swing set out back, use those as well. You can also video her putting on makeup, doing her hair, brushing her teeth. Lots of possibilities for funny commentary there.

Breakfast Treat

- After you've embarrassed the student, give him or her a chance to shower and get dressed. Make it up to the kid by taking him or her with you to wake up the next kid and then take both out to breakfast, your treat. Plan enough time, so they're not late for school.

Stage It

- If the actual wake-up was just not that funny and the student didn't respond at all, consider staging a funnier wake-up. Ask the kid to join in on the joke and pretend to be asleep and refilm the video. This is a last resort, but one I've had to use on a few occasions—particularly one time when a kid cussed me out during the initial wake-up.

Video Help

- Get your middle or high school friends, who are way more tech savvy than you are, to edit the video. It will save you a couple hours and give him or her ownership and leadership. Instruct the student to make the edited video shorter than five minutes; three minutes is ideal to keep kids wanting more and to be sure it's not too long. This might mean leaving out some funny footage, but that's OK—select the funniest, and keep it short!

- Ask your volunteer editor to use appropriate background music in the video. Instruct the student on when you need the actual video footage sound, when you need background music, or both.
- Double it up as some great contact work time by asking that person to teach you how to edit the video. Sit with him while he does it and shows you how.

Midnight Run

- If you have early-morning jobs that prevent you from doing this, consider doing a midnight run and wake the kids shortly after they have gone to bed. It doesn't have to be on a school day or night, but those are usually the safest bets to ensure they'll be asleep and not at a friend's house. The viewers will still think it's early in the morning. I have also woken a kid up at nine o'clock on a Saturday morning and set the clock in the room we filmed in for four fifteen in the morning to make it look like it was very early. We filmed the outside scene a different night in front of the house when it was dark, and inside it didn't matter.

Social Media

- Create suspense on your social media accounts. Post clues as to who might be next or clips from the full video they will see at your weekly gathering.

Big Ending

- A good way to end the semester is by staging the final wake-up where some seniors gather all of the kids who have been woken up during the semester and go and wake up the leaders who have been doing the wake-ups. This should be the most brutal wake-up. Possibly take the leaders outside, duct tape them to a tree, and spray them with the water hose.

ACKNOWLEDGMENTS

HERE'S TO "pointing to the passers." Thank you to the dozens of folks who came alongside me during this process. You all helped squeeze these words from a person to a page.

To the team at New Growth Press: Barbara Juliani, Ruth Castle, Tom Temple, Cheryl White, Gretchen Logterman, Carl Simmons, Mark and Karen Teears, John Walt, and Emily Petrini. Thank you for taking a chance on me and walking alongside me with great patience. I feel as if you're the medical team in our delivery room, and I just want to hug you all now that the book baby has finally arrived!

To the friends who gave me peaceful places to write: The Wolfes; Charlie Heritage; Justin, Jonathan, and Anne Smith; and Dr. Louis Canino, Ann Bauer, and the staff at St. Francis Springs Prayer Center. Without you all, this ADHD author would've been completely doomed.

To the advisors who offered wisdom and edits during the book writing process: Fil Anderson; Jim Hundley; Jerome Daley; Nathan Hedman; Bill and Joann Goans; Curtis Chesney; Eloise Porter; Emily Hull; my dad, Doug; and my brother, Blake, who was the Mickey to my Rocky. Your feedback was invaluable.

To the community who walks alongside us on a regular basis: Our small group (Chesneys, Whitworths, Smiths, and Heritages), our Redeemer church staff and youth volunteers (Hawkins, Meriwethers, Drakes, Lovejoys, Renslows, Webers, Hocutts, Myers, Van Wyks, Walls, Fissels, Van Wagenens, Harrises, Wests, Wises, Coxes, Stanleys, Hedmans, Lewkowiczes, Valerie Sagero, and Graham Monroe), the TCS board (Sassers and Dukes), my Young Life staff community (Terry Swenson, Steve Gardner, David Page, and Stacey Greene), and my monthly burrito bowl buddy, Dave Reule. You are friends who have become family.

To my own youth leaders, pastors, and Young Life staff during my teenage years: Truett Williams, David Thompson, Sterling Griggs, Will Toburen,

Dr. Mark Corts, Dr. Gary Chapman, Lynn Barclay Brewer, Bart Scarborough, Hunter Lambeth, and Ty Saltzgiver. Bless you all. I know I was a handful.

To my extended family: Mom and Dad; Abby, Allan, Bennett, and Lucas; Blake, Ashley, Kessler and Crosby; Nate, Suellen, Pierce, Creed, and Selwyn; Mary Leonard, Mamaw Craft, Mamaw Pumpkin, Crafts, Coleys, Clays, Minceys, Ludwigs, and Leonards. I wouldn't want to eat eight gallons of homemade ice cream with anyone else.

To my home squad: Natalie, Honey, Hutch, and Macy Heart. You have all made countless sacrifices so these pages could be written. You are each a constant reminder of God's grace to me. I find such great delight in you! If, for some crazy reason, a *whole lot* of people buy this book, I'll take you to Disney World.

And to my Abba Father, my brother Jesus, and the Holy Spirit—O, how you have loved me through the writing of the words. There is none like You.

ENDNOTES

Introduction
[1] Jack Miller, founder of Serge (formerly World Harvest Mission) and the New Life Presbyterian network of churches, was well known for giving this summation of the gospel.

Chapter 1
[1] Linda (Medill) MacDonald, "Broken Heart," *Linda J. MacDonald* (blog), https://www.lindajmacdonald.com/broken-heart-play.

[2] This is a term borrowed from Carl Jung's archetypal dynamics and is expounded on in a spiritual context in Henri Nouwen's *The Wounded Healer: Ministry in Contemporary Society* (New York: Doubleday Image Books, 1979).

Chapter 2
[1] Ed Cash, "S.O.S.," 2012. Used throughout this chapter, with permission from Ed Cash.

Chapter 4
[1] The movie is called *Courageous* (directed by Alex Kendrick; Sherwood Pictures, 2011), and I know lots of people who love it and others who hate it. This is not an endorsement to see it, but if you search YouTube for "Courageous opening scene," it's pretty powerful.

[2] Sally Lloyd-Jones, *The Jesus Storybook Bible* (Grand Rapids: Zonderkidz, 2007), 20.

Chapter 8
[1] David Paul Kirkpatrick, "Jesus' Bachelors," *David Paul Kirkpatrick's Living in the Metaverse* (blog), March 25, 2013, http://www.davidpaulkirkpatrick.com/2013/03/25/jesus-bachelors-the-disciples-were-most-likely-under-the-age-of-18.

[2] Paul Miller, *Love Walked Among Us: Learning to Love Like Jesus* (Colorado Springs: NavPress, 2001), 245.

[3] Rebecca Pippert, *Out of the Saltshaker & Into the World* (Downers Grove, IL: InterVarsity, 1999), 11.

Chapter 9
[1] Lloyd-Jones, *The Jesus Storybook Bible*, 14–17.

Part Three
[1] Eugene Peterson, *The Jesus Way: A Conversation on the Ways That Jesus Is the Way* (London: Hodder & Stoughton, 2007), 22.

Chapter 11

[1] William Hazlitt, *The Collected Works of William Hazlitt: Fugitive Writings* (London: J. M. Dent & Company, 1904), 447.

Chapter 12

[1] Henri J. M. Nouwen, *Gracias!: A Latin American Journal* (New York: Harper & Row, 1983), 147.

Chapter 13

[1] Used with permission. Sandra McCracken, Album: Psalms, track 2, 2015.

[2] Ruth MacKay, "What's for Dinner?" *Interaction: Stanford University News* 9 (Spring 2008): 2–10, https://news.stanford.edu/news/multi/pdf/multi_9sm.pdf.

[3] Leonard Sweet, *From Tablet to Talk* (Carol Stream: NavPress, 2015), 10.

[4] Ibid., 11.

[5] Douglas McKelvey, *Every Moment Holy* (Nashville: Rabbit Room Press, 2017), 112–15.

Chapter 14

[1] Jim Branch, "Let's Change Pants," The *Young Life Leader Blog*, August 31, 2016, http://www.younglifeleaders.org/2016/08/lets-change-pants.html.

Chapter 15

[1] Ray Williams, "8 Reasons Why We Need Human Touch More Than Ever," *Psychology Today*, March 28, 2015, https://www.psychologytoday.com/blog/wired-success/201503/8-reasons-why-we-need-human-touch-more-ever.

[2] "haptomai," Bible Hub, http://biblehub.com/greek/680.htm.

[3] Drew Hill, "A Powerful Way to Honor Your Graduating Students," *Young Life Leader Blog*, April 18, 2017, http://www.younglifeleaders.org/2017/04/a-powerful-way-to-honor-your-graduating.html.

[4] Williams, "8 Reasons Why We Need Human Touch."

[5] Drew Hill, "Let's Come Up with a Handshake," *Young Life Leader Blog*, August 26, 2016, http://www.younglifeleaders.org/2016/08/lets-come-up-with-handshake.html.

Chapter 17

[1] Elizabeth J. W. Spencer, "Stealing the Silver," *Making Me Brave* (blog), June 19, 2016, http://www.makingmebrave.com/blog-posts/2016/5/25/part-3-of-3-tradition-silver-candlesticks.

[2] Quoted in Mike Mason, *Practicing the Presence of People: How We Learn to Love* (Colorado Springs: Waterbrook, 1999), 53.

[3] C. S. Lewis, *Mere Christianity* (New York: Touchstone, 1996), 175–76.

[4] J. D. Grear, *Gaining by Losing: Why the Future Belongs to Churches that Send* (Grand Rapids: Zondervan, 2015), 29.

[5] Text: Irish poem; trans. Mary E. Byrne, 1905; vers. Eleanor Hull, 1912, alt.

Chapter 18

[1] Merilyn Hargis, "On the Road," *Christian History* 59 (1998): 26, https://christianhistoryinstitute.org/magazine/issue/life-and-times-of-jesus-of-nazareth.

Chapter 19

[1] "BookBrowse's Favorite Quotes," BookBrowse, https://www.bookbrowse.com/quotes/detail/index.cfm/quote_number/401/if-you-want-to-build-a-ship-dont-drum-up-people-but-rather-teach-them-to-long-for-the-endless-immensity-of-the-sea.

Chapter 20

[1] Rev. Dr. Kwame O. Lartey, *Fervent and Effective Prayers: For Every Day in the Week from Sunday to Saturday* (Bloomington: Xlibris, 2009), 24.

Chapter 21

[1] Henri J. M. Nouwen, *Bread for the Journey: A Daybook of Wisdom and Faith* (San Francisco: HarperOne, 2006), 46.

[2] Jason Headley, "It's Not about the Nail," YouTube, 1:41, May 22, 2013, https://www.youtube.com/watch?v=-4EDhdAHrOg.

[3] Amy Piatt and Christian Piatt, *MySpace to Sacred Space: God for a New Generation* (Danvers: Chalice Press, 2007), 159–60. Note that each paragraph of the quote represents a separate thought from this section and that they do not necessarily follow sequentially as they do in the Piatts' book.

[4] Jason Gray, "Not Right Now, the Story Behind the Song," *Jason Gray Music* (blog), March 6, 2014, https://jasongraymusic.wordpress.com/2014/03/06/not-right-now-the-story-behind-the-song.

Chapter 22

[1] "Tetelestai—Paid in Full," *Precept Austin* (blog), April 21, 2017, http://www.preceptaustin.org/tetelestai-paid_in_full.

[2] Charles Spurgeon, quoted by Erwin W. Lutzer in *Cries from the Cross: A Journey into the Heart of Jesus* (Chicago: Moody Publishers, 2015), 127.

Chapter 23

[1] Richard J. Foster, *Prayer: Finding the Heart's True Home* (San Francisco: HarperOne, 2003), 192.

[2] Dietrich Bonhoeffer, *Life Together: The Classic Exploration of Christian Community* (London: SCM Press, 2015), 112.

Chapter 24

[1] Idea borrowed from James Bryan Smith, *The Good and Beautiful God: Falling in Love with the God Jesus Already Knows* (Downers Grove, IL: InterVarsity, 2009), 185.

[2] Sean Casey, "2016 Nielsen Social Media Report," *Nielsen.com* (blog), January 17, 2017, http://www.nielsen.com/us/en/insights/reports/2017/2016-nielsen-social-media-report.html.

[3] Jim Rayburn III, *From Bondage to Liberty: Dance, Children, Dance* (Colorado Springs: Morningstar Press, 2000), 47–49.

Chapter 25
[1] Paul Miller, *Love Walked Among Us: Learning to Love Like Jesus.*

[2] John Ortberg, *If You Want to Walk on Water, You've Got to Get Out of the Boat* (Grand Rapids: Zondervan, 2001), 9.

[3] Gary Chapman, *The 5 Love Languages: The Secret to Love That Lasts* (Chicago: Northfield Publishing, 1992).

Chapter 26
[1] *Diagnostic and Statistical Manual of Mental Disorders*, 5th ed., DSM-5. (Lake St. Louis: American Psychiatric Association, 2013).

Chapter 27
[1] Mike Barnett and William R. Yount, *Called to Reach: Equipping Cross-cultural Disciplers* (Nashville: B&H Publishing Group, 2007), 53.

[2] Shane Claiborne, *The Irresistible Revolution: Living as an Ordinary Radical*, 10th ed. (Grand Rapids: Zondervan, 2016), 174.

[3] Excerpts from Elton Trueblood in *The Best of Elton Trueblood* ed. James R. Newby (Nashville: Impact Books, 1979).

Chapter 28
[1] Craig L. Blomberg, *1 Corinthians: The NIV Application Commentary* (Grand Rapids: Zondervan, 2009), 217.

[2] Douglas McKelvey, *Every Moment Holy.*

Chapter 29
[1] Wendell Berry, *Jayber Crow* (Berkeley: Counterpoint Press, 2001), 12.

[2] Jim Rayburn's prayer adaptation, quoted by Jeff Chesemore in *Made for This: The Young Life Story* (Colorado Springs: Young Life, 2015), 65.